The Nazi/Skokie Conflict

David Hamlin

The Nazi/Skokie Conflict

A Civil Liberties Battle

Beacon Press   Boston

Portions of this book appeared, in somewhat different form, in *The Civil Liberties Review.*

Copyright © 1980 by David Hamlin
Beacon Press books are published under the auspices of The Unitarian Universalist Association, 25 Beacon Street, Boston, MA 02108.

Published simultaneously in Canada by
Fitzhenry & Whiteside Limited, Toronto

Printed in the United States of America

(hardcover) 9 8 7 6 5 4 3 2 1
(paperback) 9 8 7 6 5 4 3 2 1

Library of Congress Cataloging in Publication Data

Hamlin, David, 1945–
        The Nazi/Skokie conflict.

        1. Liberty of speech — United States. 2. Assembly,
Right of — United States. 3. National Socialist Party
of America. 4. American Civil Liberties Union.
5. Skokie, Ill. — Demonstration, 1977. I. Title.
KF4772.H36   342.73′085   80-68165
ISBN 0-8070-3230-1

ah, but in such a time
of ugliness
   the true protest
    is beauty
     —Phil Ochs

Acknowledgements

The author is most grateful for the aid, comfort, and assistance provided during the events described in this book by Franklyn Haiman, Edwin Rothschild, Wilson McDermut, Sheila Meyer, Tina Adachi, Odell Hayes, Trude Schutz, Lois Lipton, Barbara O'Toole, Sheila Insley, Jean Snyder, Dawn Ragan, Dorothy Burstein, Paul Gross, Howard Hawhee, Nancy Rosen, Babs Joseph, and the incomparable David Goldberger.

Special thanks as well to Diane Cleaver, Joan and Jim Ashley (for wasping around), the Wednesday Evening Players Association, Sydney Weisman, and Jason B. Hamlin.

Contents

The First Amendment:
Congress shall make no law respecting an establishment of religion, or prohibiting the free exercise thereof; or abridging the freedom of speech, or of the press; or the right of the people peaceably to assemble, and to petition the government for a redress of grievances.

1

Swastikas

Frank Collin is a citizen of the United States. He is also a Fascist, a racist, and a self-avowed Nazi. Collin heads the National Socialist Party of America, a Chicago-based Neo-Nazi organization, which he himself founded. Through NSPA, he advocates a doctrine of supreme evil: Frank Collin would forcibly deport all blacks, Jews, and Latinos. To obliterate opposition, he would replace liberty with tyranny. He would supplant justice and law with a whimsical, vicious system of inequity, a system calculated to outlaw equality and punish tolerance. He would destroy freedom.

Collin's doctrine is one of brutality and fear and hatred. It thrives on persecution and degradation as it strives toward its loathsome goal, a "master race." It is the doctrine of Adolf Hitler — barely disguised — and once served as the cornerstone for a government built on terror, insanity, and murder. It is a doctrine of awesome enormity. Nazism evokes the most vivid of memories and the most shattering of fears. It is an ideological nightmare full of darkness, distortion, and dread.

Frank Collin has adopted the symbols of that doctrine. His followers wear brown shirts, black boots, and swastika armbands, while Collin himself wears in addition several more swastikas, including one on his belt buckle, and a faintly Hitlerian haircut. When he goes into the streets—

with the symbols, venom, and uniformed followers — the results are inevitably dramatic.

Frank Collin, standing before his troops, seems to be a dangerous, charismatic dynamo, exhorting his followers to roll over entire populations and crush everything in their way. The members of the National Socialist Party of America resemble true stormtroopers, disciplined and poised to knock on the door in a brutal search for "undesirables." America's consistent, determined rejection of all that Frank Collin represents seems to vanish into thin air, replaced as if by magic with cries of "It *can* happen here" and a panicked, contagious vision of fascism, in which Collin sweeps into power before anyone notices.

It is all an illusion.

Frank Collin is a dull, inept, unimposing man. In public he is a poor, woefully ineffective speaker who backs up his ravings with one-page, childlike cartoon propaganda. Beyond the public's eye, he is, if anything, slower and duller. Frank Collin leaves the distinct impression that he is incapable of leading a parade through a tunnel without losing his way; he is so confused by the alterations he himself has made in his own doctrine that he forgets who the "enemy" is.

Frank Collin sits atop an organization that is all façade. The very best estimates of NSPA's membership — estimates made by those with the greatest stake in monitoring Collin's strength — run no higher than two dozen. The financial base of the organization is so thin that the telephone at NSPA headquarters is as often as not disconnected for failure to pay the bill. The only real distinction Collin's organization enjoys is the name: NSPA is the most dishonestly named organization in the nation.

The National Socialist Party of America is not national. Collin rarely ventures beyond his neighborhood in southwest Chicago, and even then he goes no farther afield than St. Louis or southern Wisconsin. Nor is NSPA socialist. Although it shares the use of that word with virtually every other Neo-Nazi group in America, NSPA bears no more allegiance to true socialism than it does to any other egalitarian philosophy. The National Socialist Party of America is a "party" only if a group with a marked lack of members, severely limited financial resources, and the utter absence of any electoral success whatsoever qualifies for the designation. Collin's organization is, finally, only "of America" in a purely chimerical sense.

Beneath that pretentious façade lie disorganization, ineptitude, and folly. When Collin is not available, press statements from NSPA are made by whoever gets to the telephone first. As a consequence, an underling (presumably *not* following orders) once announced to the world a rally — complete with time, place, and date — which Collin himself had apparently never even imagined, much less approved.

The dreaded brutal Fascists Collin leads are in fact young street kids who are rarely brutal and hardly dreadful, and whose arrest records run to disorderly conduct born of an occasional street scuffle. More often than not they content themselves with shouting their taunts from behind the relative security provided by massive Chicago Police Department protection.

Such bravado is not surprising from an organization led by a man whose finest hour as a street brawler speaks volumes about his real courage. In the aftermath of a sudden attack by a band of anti-Fascists on his party

3

headquarters, Collin found that one of the raiding party had been left behind. In the safety of his own headquarters, surrounded by his own followers, Frank Collin managed to beat — and hurt — the lone woman trapped inside. If he is going to rise to power on the backs of his opponents, Frank Collin will evidently have to lure them into his headquarters, one at a time, to do it.

Outside the NSPA headquarters, Collin and his followers meet everything except support. His rallies draw opponents, always in numbers far in excess of Collin's own. His rallies draw the curious: toughs — from Jewish Defense League members to the guys from the corner bar willing to swing at anybody — and lots and lots of police, who protect Collin. But almost always, when Frank Collin faces an audience, his followers are behind him.

Although Frank Collin is, indeed, a hopeless leader with a helpless cause, his sudden rise to power is openly anticipated by many of his opponents. While barely able to manage his own existence, he can command press coverage reaching around the world. Frank Collin and his followers constitute nothing more than a comic charade on their very best days, yet their opposition would change democracy itself rather than give them a forum.

Such is the power of Frank Collin's illusion that Collin himself seems to become important and successful and capable. In fact he is none of those things.

The illusion rests on the symbols of nazism. Without those symbols, Frank Collin would not merit a second glance. With them, however, Collin accomplishes exactly the same result that any good magician attains: misdirection. The audience's attention is misdirected, forced away from reality and toward the illusion, by the symbols of fascism.

Thus, the petty criminals and cowards of NSPA are transformed by the swastika into the image of stormtroopers, and the nearly total lack of support within America for NSPA turns into the dreadful image of tens of thousands of Nazis, stiff-armed and organized.

The power of those images is such that the audience begins, almost immediately, to concentrate on them. The concentration grows with each new recollection and each newly awakened fear until, at last, the awesome enormity of nazism becomes the only thing the audience sees at all. The misdirection becomes complete, and therefore completely effective, when the two images blur into one. So the illusion was perfectly executed, once, when a news report on a Chicago television station featured a story concerning Frank Collin's Chicago activities with a film of the excavation of a Nazi death camp, film that was shot before Frank Collin was born.

When the illusion is that complete, Frank Collin truly appears to be all of the things he is not. While that is a truly remarkable feat, it does not imply that Frank Collin is, ultimately, a cunning manipulator of media and emotion. That would be true were it not for a single, stunning fact: Frank Collin's illusion is intended for an audience of one — it is created for the exclusive benefit of Frank Collin himself. Any others who see the performance are secondary.

The only person Collin wants to misdirect is Collin himself. It is Frank Collin whom Collin confuses and tricks, for it is Frank Collin whom Collin wants to misdirect away from reality.

Frank Collin is Jewish. He is Frank Cohn, the son of a survivor of the Nazi holocaust. He is the child of a death camp refugee. The fact is beyond dispute. It is confirmed by sources as divergent as the Federal Bureau of Investigation and one of Chicago's finest journalists. Frank Collin protests that it is not so — he rants and raves at reporters who bring it up in his presence — but even other Nazi organizations in the Chicago area shun him; nobody believes his protests.

The FBI disclosed Collin's background through an ugly and unreliable program known as COINTELPRO. COINTELPRO is FBI-ese for COunter INTELligence PROgram, and it was created to monitor — and then to harass, disrupt, infiltrate, abuse, and destroy — dissident political movements in America. Through COINTELPRO, the FBI did everything it could to create chaos, mistrust, and failure among political groups outside the mainstream. For the most part, COINTELPRO operations were confined to the left, but Collin somehow became a target as well — perhaps because he turned out to be such an easy mark.

Frank Collin was, at the time, a member of the national American Nazi Party, headed by the notorious George Lincoln Rockwell. When the FBI discovered and released Frank Collin-Cohn's birth certificate, Collin was instantly ousted. He promptly founded NSPA. Thus, there resulted the sort of outcome which only the FBI could revere, in which two Fascist organizations were created when only one had existed before.

Whatever the strange fruit of the FBI's efforts, the methods are obviously suspect. Indeed, one facet of COINTELPRO was the conscious creation of *false* information, a tactic which the FBI called "disinformation." Such lying might occur in the form of a memo, duplicated on stolen stationery, calling on a peace group's membership to rally at the local post office on Tuesday when the rally was in fact scheduled for Wednesday or not at all.

It is possible, then, that the FBI fabricated Frank Collin's birth certificate. It is not plausible, however, because such an act would imply a certain finesse, a flair, absent from everything else the FBI did in that period or since, from finding Patricia Hearst to halting the antiwar movement dead in its tracks.

It would be unfair, of course, to assume that the FBI made up everything. It seems far more likely that the FBI simply realized that they had found a good thing. In any event, the FBI's disclosure has since been confirmed by reporters with none of the suspect motives imputable to the actions of the FBI.

Among those journalists is Chicago's Mike Royko, whose national reputation as a champion of the common man, a biting wit, and a deadly accurate biographer of Richard Daley obscures his local reputation as a fine street reporter. Royko investigated and reported Collin's ancestry in typically barbed style, urging Collin's opponents who line the routes of his marches to shout, "So's your old man!"

The humor makes the fact no less reliable, and Royko's work has been confirmed by still other reporters. In one such instance, a reporter actually located Collin's parents, who told him that Frank Collin had forbidden them to discuss the matter, which is surely the ultimate confirmation.

The illusion that surrounds Frank Collin, then, is only a device designed to convince Collin that he is all of the things he is not. For when Frank Collin degrades and defiles Jews, Frank Cohn silently suffers self-inflicted wounds.

7

When Frank Cohn remembers his childhood, Frank Collin betrays his cause. When Frank Collin tries to intimidate his enemies, Frank Cohn cowers. When Frank Cohn wants to go home, Frank Collin is lost.

The entire illusion rests on the symbols of fascism, symbols which make the trick effective. But the illusion exists because Frank Collin is, by his own stated definition, his own worst enemy. It is because Frank Collin is also Frank Cohn that this inept, unimposing failure wraps himself in the fabric of fabrication — cloaks himself in the trappings of nazism — and creates an illusion in which Frank Collin-Cohn seems to become everything, literally *everything*, he is not.

However bizarre the reasons or aberrant the result, Frank Collin's illusion serves to transform Collin, as if by magic, from a Hitlerian clown into a Hitler clone. The clown may not be worth much attention, but the clone almost destroyed American democracy.

Frank Collin and his National Socialist Party of America operate out of the party's headquarters on the southwest side of Chicago. The NSPA headquarters are in a neighborhood known as Marquette Park. The neighborhood takes its name from the actual park — an expanse of lawns, picnic areas, and sports facilities owned and governed by the City of Chicago's Park District — which the neighborhood surrounds. Until Collin and NSPA were locked out of both the park and the neighborhood, Marquette Park was the closest thing Frank Collin had found to natural turf.

Marquette Park is torn with urban strife. It is a neighborhood — common to cities like Boston and Philadelphia and Newark — in which sharply defined ethnic borderlines have existed for generations. Against those borderlines push black families seeking homes away from the inner city and, therefore, away from the accumulated ravages of decades of racism and neglect.

Black unemployment in Chicago is staggering, and it is worst in the inner city. Educational facilities in Chicago are badly segregated in the most tolerant neighborhoods and virtually useless in the nonwhite ghettos. Official Chicago has adopted a position of benign neglect toward black-on-black crime, a policy which is almost as merciless as the crime itself. The black families who want to move into the neighborhood of Marquette Park seek escape from that horror, and they understand that they have an absolute moral and legal right to do so.

The black families edging toward Marquette Park do not encounter white sheriffs with cattle prods or hooded vigilantes; they encounter white freedom fighters, people whose commitment to freedom differs in form from the black commitment but is no less strongly felt. The whites of Marquette Park are, in large part, immigrants from countries now under Communist domination. They seek to preserve their culture and their heritage in order to be sure that both will one day return home safely.

So, for example, when the Lithuanian community of Marquette Park holds a cultural celebration in the picnic area of their park, it is less a celebration of that culture than it is a fierce display of resistance, a determined show of pride, a taunt to the Communist dominators.

While the impact of the white attitudes in Marquette Park is not markedly different from other such racial confrontations — each side views the other with fear, distrust, and hostility — the reasons for this particular confrontation make resolution impossible. To honor the black right to move would threaten the white right to fight back (at least in the eyes of the white community, which also holds "ethnic purity" in its more racist sense equally dear). Similarly, to honor the whites' resistance efforts would deny basic rights to the blacks.

In the middle of that conflict — and at the virtual core of the tensions which that conflict has generated — is the NSPA headquarters. On the borderline between the white neighborhoods and the black migration sits Frank Collin's office. On the side of the building, in large letters, is Collin's message to his community: "NIGGER GO HOME."

The problems which created the conflict in Marquette Park have existed for years. So have Frank Collin's inflammatory demonstrations, black civil-rights marches, "community" efforts on all sides, and growing tension. The City of Chicago, faced with all of that, did nothing. It was not until the summer of 1976, when the tension reached a peak, that official Chicago took any action at all.

Frank Collin's parades and rallies in the Marquette Park area were sprawling, noisy affairs. Through the summer of 1976, Collin's calls to "drive back the nigger" fell on the ears of young white boys, bored with summer and receptive to Collin's call because of their parents' fears.

At the same time, black civil-rights leaders staged rallies and demonstrations in Marquette Park and the surrounding neighborhood. Although the larger, more powerful civil-rights groups — groups such as the Urban League, NAACP, and Chicago's own Operation PUSH — shunned both the conflict in the neighborhood and the black leadership in that conflict, the black rallies still drew sizable crowds.

10

By the end of the summer, rock-throwing incidents were common. Gangs of white kids roamed the streets, and police began to discover caches of rocks in alleys and on rooftops. At least one black minister involved in the civil-rights demonstrations talked with deadly conviction about the effect on an enemy's skull of an army surplus jacket, the pockets of which have been filled with stones. The tensions of Marquette Park had spilled into the streets, and the City of Chicago — responding to the tensions — finally took action.

In the offices of the City of Chicago — in the police department, in city hall, in the Chicago Park District — the First Amendment to the United States Constitution is thought to be an unverified rumor. Only under the most dire of circumstances will the City of Chicago recognize citizens' rights to freedom of expression.

Official Chicago's antipathy toward free speech is a rich tradition. From the earliest days of machine politics in Chicago until long after the world had seen what Chicago's mayor thought about free speech and assembly during the 1968 Democratic Convention, the regular Democratic machine which had controlled Chicago had also controlled speech in Chicago.

Dr. Martin Luther King, Jr., antiwar demonstrators, labor organizers, Iranian students, religious cultists, leafleteers and pamphleteers, street preachers, abortion opponents and pro-choice advocates, mothers, ministers, or Maoists: *nobody* communicates an idea in Chicago without enduring a major hassle first.

The bureaucratic minefield that constitutes Chicago's rules and regulations for demonstrating is alone enough to stifle all but the most dedicated demonstrators and

11

speakers. The City of Chicago once tied up plans for a pro-Equal Rights Amendment rally for days while the city's lawyers argued with the women staging the demonstration over a single, minuscule point: what to do if any of the women slipped off the curb and onto the street. The City of Chicago can bounce demonstrators seeking permits from one agency to another with remarkable facility, sending organizers from city hall to the police department to the park district and back in search of a permit which may not be required in the first place.

If those seeking permission to express an idea in Chicago can negotiate the maze the city has built, they win only permission, and the city has ways of foiling even permitted demonstrations. A group opposing nuclear proliferation once tried to negotiate Chicago's permit puzzle in order to stage a rally on the grounds of Chicago's famous landmark, the Water Tower. When they failed to solve the permit puzzle, the group sought relief in federal court, where they won the right to demonstrate. By the time the court's order had been issued, the park surrounding the Water Tower had been completely excavated by the city, and there was not an inch of level ground left within shouting distance of the tower. The city denied any relationship between the court action and the excavation.

Even when Chicago's officials react less dramatically and even when would-be demonstrators are persistent enough to avoid all the land mines, the right to free speech in Chicago is by no means secure. More than one group has secured a permit and held a permitted demonstration under the watchful eyes of the Chicago police only to have the same police arrest the demonstrators ten minutes after they have begun for "disorderly conduct" or "disobeying an officer."

Taking the City of Chicago to court to secure freedoms may be slightly more effective than trying to outfox the city's officials, but it is no less arduous a task. Chicago has an army of lawyers, an army which tends to send in a battalion where a raw recruit would do. In addition, Chicago appeals *everything,* thus consuming time and money and energy. The city once took to the United States Supreme Court on appeal the incredible contention that the Chicago police had an unfettered right to infiltrate teams of lawyers whose "crime" was to sue the city.

Where the army of trial lawyers fails, the army of draftsmen lawyers does not. Chicago's army is as adept at semantic warfare as it is at court battling, and as often as not a city ordinance declared unconstitutional will quickly re-emerge in a new, if only subtly changed, variation. Thus, when a federal judge voided, on First Amendment grounds, a Chicago prostitution ordinance, the lawyer army drafted a new one, the city council passed it, and within a matter of weeks the police were engaging in precisely the same tactics that had led to the litigation in the first place.

A very simple principle lies at the base of Chicago's massive effort to thwart even the most benign speech: the easiest way to retain political power is to eliminate, or reduce to total ineffectiveness, all opposition. The City of Chicago's political machine has always understood that once the Nazis are free to communicate the Republicans will probably try it too. While the city recognizes the true spirit of the First Amendment's guarantee, that speech and

13

assembly are free to all citizens, it views that lofty principle as a contemptible annoyance.

Because of that antidemocratic tradition, official Chicago took notice of the tensions and the troubles in Marquette Park. The City of Chicago responded to the situation in the neighborhood by shutting down the park to all demonstrators, by trying to bar Collin entirely, and by finding an old park district ordinance that was flagrantly unconstitutional and, therefore, perfectly suited to the city's needs.

Oddly, the one thing which Chicago might have done to ease the tensions in Marquette Park was the only thing Chicago is absolutely unwilling to do. The city could have recognized the full value of the First Amendment and used that value to advantage. Chicago might have issued permits to all sides in the Marquette Park controversy, allowing everyone a chance to be heard, while using judicious police presence to control both the actions and reactions. It is possible that such a program — in addition to easing the tensions by allowing some steam to be blown off — might even have helped both sides understand the other's point of view.

To ease the tensions in that way, of course, would have forced Chicago to recognize both Frank Collin's and the civil-rights advocates' right to free speech. In short, it would have been the functional equivalent of dismantling Chicago's Democratic machine — the regular Democrats of Cook County, Illinois, do not go about cutting their own throats.

But the City of Chicago did not take advantage of the First Amendment. Instead, it responded in its traditional way and sought to stifle dissent on all sides in Marquette

Park. In the opening gambit, the city took Frank Collin to court. Chicago charged, in effect, that there was so much turmoil surrounding Collin's demonstrations that he should be censored. Ignoring both Collin's right to freedom of speech and assembly and its own responsibility to protect those freedoms, Chicago asked the court to rule Collin illegal, to ban him from demonstrating. The court, however, denied the city's request.

At the same time, however, permits to use Marquette Park itself had become as scarce as Republicans on Chicago's payrolls. Civil-rights groups found that the park district was making it difficult, if not impossible, to secure the right to demonstrate in the park. While the civil-rights groups met with their lawyers to try to sort out the latest requirements for demonstrations in Marquette Park, Frank Collin exercised a permit, issued months before, to demonstrate there.

Where the city's lawyers and bureaucracy had failed, the Chicago police did not. Collin followed a route dictated to him by the police, the identical route he had followed on police orders the last time he had marched in the neighborhood. On this occasion, however, the police stopped him when he reached a crossing point on the route. Although the situation was under control and there was a massive police force in and around the area, the officer in charge ordered Collin to turn back his march, and he ordered the patrolmen standing by to arrest Collin if he said "anything derogatory" while informing the marchers of the change.

Collin turned to face his followers; he spoke no more than a dozen words before he disappeared under a sea of arresting officers. He had, in fact, been delivering the message he had been ordered to deliver. He had, in fact,

15

violated no law at all. He was, in fact, arrested anyhow. It was sometime later before a Cook County judge found Collin innocent of any unlawful conduct, but that hardly changed the fact that Collin had been stopped cold in the neighborhood where Chicago wanted no action.

Collin's arrest and the earlier court action against him as well as the evasive tactics which the civil-rights groups met all served the same short-term purpose: to keep Marquette Park quiet. To guarantee that tranquillity, or at least to prolong the appearance of it, Chicago also had a long-term weapon, a veritable giant-killer.

From the offices of the Chicago Park District came a new (or newly discovered) requirement: any group wishing to assemble in the parks of Chicago would be required to post in advance a bond or insurance policy in the amount of two hundred and fifty thousand dollars. Never known for action taken by half-measures, the Chicago Park District had placed a price tag on "free assembly" of one quarter of a million dollars *per demonstration.*

Obviously, none but the most wealthy and tame of demonstrations would ever get into the parks. The general air of tension and trouble surrounding Marquette Park would send any sensible insurance agent running for cover, and neither Collin nor the black groups could find anything approaching the sort of cash required for a bond. Moreover, even where insurance companies might be willing to write a policy of the sort Chicago required, the cost would be as high as a bond fee and equally unreachable.

By trapping potential demonstrators between a huge price tag on one hand and the inherent conservative nature of the insurance industry on the other, the park district enabled itself to refuse to issue permits on a regular basis.

The scheme had a minor flaw: it was thoroughly illegal. With an army of lawyers ready to do battle, however, even that flaw turned to Chicago's advantage.

To expose the flaw, somebody would have to take the Chicago Park District to court. The only way to do that would be to cross the threshold of the Federal Court Building in Chicago. Across that threshold lie continuances and delays, motions and countermotions, briefs and reply-briefs, and calendars so backlogged that even the simplest act takes five, ten, twenty times longer than necessary.

The Chicago Park District's officials and lawyers had concocted an almost perfect scheme: no permits to demonstrate would be issued until and unless the demonstrators could prove that they had insurance, which was impossible to obtain. The only way into Chicago's parks was through the courtroom, where Chicago's army of lawyers waited.

The park district scheme was so successful, in fact, that Frank Collin's late-summer demonstration in 1976 was the last such activity in Marquette Park for almost two years.

By the time the Chicago Park District's quarter-million-dollar insurance requirement had silenced the city's parks, including Marquette, Frank Collin already had a keen understanding of First Amendment rights. Collin is no scholar, legal or otherwise, but he has developed shrewd survival instincts — a kind of street savvy — and knew immediately that the requirement was illegal.

Over the years, Collin had marched and demonstrated and rallied and campaigned and picketed and shouted. As often as not, his attempts to engage in any of those activities met with censorship. On special occasions, Collin would meet an act of censorship devised exclusively for him (as, for example, the exotic suit by the City of Chicago to ban Collin outright). In every instance, Collin had found that the First Amendment would protect him so long as he remained within the boundaries of criminal law. Since street action is at the heart of Frank Collin's activities, the lesson of all those encounters was not lost on him.

Collin offers his followers little save attention. If they follow along behind him, wearing their uniforms, Collin's followers will enjoy some press attention or, at an absolute minimum, a small but vocal audience. Since Collin offers his followers no power, no prestige, and no potential for either, the attention they get in the streets is probably their only remuneration.

Frank Collin himself has far more powerful reasons to seek the attention street action offers. An illusion performed in an empty room captures the attention of none save the illusionist. However self-serving his illusion, Collin must still have his audience. The ability to misdirect is absolutely useless unless somebody is present to follow the deception and look in the wrong direction.

To assure himself that his illusion is working, Collin must be sure that somebody, somewhere, is watching. The instincts he has developed to that end triggered a simple, direct analysis of the park district's requirement: his audience was gone. Collin moved immediately to restore it.

Frank Collin responded to the two hundred and fifty thousand dollar insurance requirement with a twenty-cent phone call. He called the American Civil Liberties Union and asked for legal assistance. He got it.

Collin v. *O'Malley,* a civil suit on behalf of Frank Collin and the National Socialist Party of America charging that the Chicago Park District insurance/bond requirement was a direct violation of the First Amendment, was filed in the United States District Court for the Northern District of Illinois in fall 1976. Collin's legal representation was provided by the Illinois Division of the ACLU, and the lawyer assigned to the case was David Goldberger, an American Jew.

The flood of contradictions created by that odd alliance may constitute one of America's most perfect ironies, but it is an irony which caused not a murmur. However ironic the association—a Fascist seeking and getting legal assistance from civil libertarians, a racist turning to a civil-rights group, an anti-Semite turning to a Jew, advocates of freedom defending freedom's enemy—not a soul in greater Chicago saw fit to comment on it.

The utter silence which greeted ACLU's litigation on behalf of Collin was caused, in part, by the commonplace nature of the event. For the better part of eight years, off and on, ACLU had represented Collin in a variety of First Amendment disputes. Most recently, ACLU had provided Collin's defense against the city's suit to ban his demonstrations altogether. That effort had, quite literally, put Frank Collin back in the streets. It is a measure of the commonplace character of such ACLU action that the previous litigation drew as little notice as the park district suit did.

Moreover, ACLU representation was both expected and accepted in Chicago on virtually all First Amendment matters, Collin's included. The tension that has developed over the years between the local ACLU and the City of Chicago is as much a part of the cityscape as Irish politicians.

19

The tension between ACLU and Chicago has its roots in a strange point of agreement between the two. ACLU members and Cook County Regular Democrats share the belief that the extension of First Amendment rights to one person or group compels that extension to all. The difference is simply that ACLU defends the principle, whereas Chicago's machine tries to beat the damn thing into submission.

Out of that tension grow all manner of odd alliances. When ACLU discovered that Chicago's political structure had been spying on virtually every political organization in the city, ACLU filed suit on behalf of virtually every political organization in the city. The suit thus joins Communists with Socialists, militant rebels with elected officeholders, lawyers with anarchists.

When Frank Collin called to seek First Amendment assistance in the insurance matter, he joined an already skewed client list. Collin lined up with a sitting Illinois legislator, a sizable number of hookers, an improbable organization known as "Jews for Jesus," and several high school students who wished to see violent movies — a catalogue of citizens with First Amendment hassles getting ACLU help.

Thus, another lawsuit on behalf of yet another censorship victim in Chicago was barely worthy of note. Indeed, the event would probably have been noteworthy only in the absence of ACLU's talents. If ACLU was representing such a broad range of political and religious points of view in free speech disputes, what difference could another odd or unpopular perspective make? However odd the irony, it drew no attention because of its common acceptance.

So the media of Chicago barely noticed the litigation

when it was filed in district court. Each of the three daily newspapers in Chicago at the time (now there are but two) had reporters assigned to the federal court beat, an assignment which is almost exclusively litigation coverage. All of the electronic outlets in Chicago (a mass of radio and television stations including three network owned-and-operated TV outlets) cover litigation as well as the print reporters do. Those reporters, however, saw fit to give the park district suit scant coverage, if any at all.

Similarly, the public showed no enthusiasm for the Collin suit. One individual — representing a senior-citizens' organization which was also locked out of the parks by the high bond — asked why her group had not been approached to file the litigation; that was the only direct response to the suit ACLU received. No community leaders threatened to pull ACLU down, no rabbis rose to excoriate ACLU or David Goldberger, no anti-Fascists occupied the ACLU offices, no ACLU members resigned or protested — the whole matter passed into the federal courts without so much as a whisper.

A few individuals did note the Collin litigation. The clerk of the United States District Court, of course, duly noted the litigation by entering it on the court's docket and assigning it a number and a judge. The officials of the Chicago Park District noted the suit as well, for they had been sued. Richard Troy learned of the suit as quickly as did the park district officers, because he is the park district's lawyer. It is entirely possible that Troy smiled upon learning of the suit.

Richard Troy belongs to Chicago's political machine. He is a lawyer-on-retainer to a number of Chicago agencies, including (but hardly limited to) the park district. When he is not serving as lawyer for the machine, Richard Troy serves it in other ways. When the Cook County Regular Democratic Organization needed a patsy to run against a powerhouse Republican attorney general, Troy was tapped for the job. He ran, quite willingly, into a predictable, inevitable crushing defeat. Moreover, in the rich tradition of Chicago politics, Troy does not leave his connections at the office: he is the son-in-law of one of Chicago's more storied — and very powerful — ward bosses.

So when Frank Collin sued the park district, he got Richard Troy in the bargain. Troy, representing an agency given to evasion and delay and continuance and misunderstanding, probably could not wait for Collin to enter the court. As soon as he did so, Collin would be exactly where the park district wanted him to be — it would be Richard Troy's job to keep him there for as long as possible.

Indeed, the clerk's docketing of the suit was a veritable flood of action compared with what would follow. The combination of the natural lethargy of the court system and the well-honed (if questionable) tactics of Troy and the park district put Collin in that most common of litigation postures: Frank Collin started to wait.

Although Collin's only goal in the lawsuit was the restoration of his audience, the suit now became a barrier to that goal. Collin waited into the new year for court action which would get him closer to Marquette Park. During all of that time — more than four months — Collin was barred from Marquette Park, and during all of that time there was no appreciable progress toward a resolution of the issues in the litigation.

By January 1977, Frank Collin faced the very real possibility that he would be off the streets and out of the parks for at least a year and perhaps much longer. Collin faced two choices. Either he could wait out the litigation in the hope that he would eventually win and be able to return to Marquette Park and his most easily accessible audience, or he could forget Marquette Park and fill the time with other activities, activities aimed at an entirely different audience.

In the service of his twisted illusion, Frank Collin selected the latter course. Convinced that the court would not put him back on his turf soon enough to suit his various needs, Frank Collin elected to take his illusion on the road. Frank Collin — locked out of Chicago's parks and faced with almost certain arrest if he tried to use Chicago's streets — elected to seek audiences outside Chicago. In February 1977, Frank Collin wrote letters to more than a dozen Chicago-area suburbs. To each suburban government, Frank Collin sent a letter requesting permission to stage a Neo-Nazi rally on the grounds of a local park.

One of these dozen letters — neatly typed on official NSPA stationery, which features a large black swastika — went to the trustees of the park district of the Village of Skokie, Illinois.

2

Survivors

Skokie, Illinois, is a suburb of Chicago, just north of the city and a few miles west of Lake Michigan. It is a bedroom community, feeding its population to the city each day on a complex of elevated lines, commuter rails, and an expressway which bisects the community.

Skokie has shopping centers, bowling alleys, hair salons, a sizable number of car dealerships, bars, restaurants, and discount stores. Skokie also has a high-volume traffic strip lined with fast-food franchises and other quick-shop chain operations, but Skokie is primarily a residential community. Its streets are lined with houses and apartment buildings.

The village has a unique architectural style, a varied collection of structures which might be called "postwar slapdash." Skokie grew in the postwar economic and population booms, and the men who built the community did so with a high regard for the enormous housing demand at the time. To accommodate as many buyers and renters as possible, extra buildings were squeezed onto some blocks, a feat accomplished by placing one or more of the buildings sideways, facing the adjacent building.

At the same time, the developers managed to bring several styles to a single street. It is therefore possible to motor through Skokie passing golden arches, large red hot-dog signs, orange and red restaurants, large well-lighted pink coffee cups, and a residential street along which sit a natural wood ranch, a white brick duplex, and a three-story apartment building with a blue and green mosaic tile façade. Perhaps because portions of Skokie are at once colorful and fanciful, the community is on occasion the butt of local humor. Folksinger Larry Rand, who grew up there, croons that Skokie "has railroad tracks and the whole town's on the other side."

The oddly eclectic architecture of Skokie at least reflects the population within, since Skokie is a community of various shadings. While throughout greater Chicago Skokie is always thought of as "predominantly Jewish," there is also a large Roman Catholic population. Several other denominations are active in the community as well, and even within the Jewish population there is rich diversity. Third-generation Jewish children in Skokie share their homes with first-generation immigrant grandparents and their schools with other Jewish children whose parents have not counted generations in a long time.

Skokie does not have as many political parties as it does churches, but it is a political mixture nonetheless. The village lies in the Tenth Illinois Congressional District, a hotbed of liberalism, yet the mayor of the village can recall pockets of support for fascism in the early days of its rise in Europe. While that distant Fascist support is hardly typical of the political perspective of the village, the tenth district is not an entirely reliable barometer either.

The tenth district, for one thing, encompasses a much larger piece of geography than Skokie alone. It includes nearby Evanston, for example. The tenth is, in fact, a creation of the Chicago Democratic machine; a device which, with remarkable success, causes liberals to beat each other's brains out every other year while the machine manages to control the remainder of the hefty Cook County congressional delegation.

So the tenth is something of a world unto itself, and Skokie's local politics are, not surprisingly, less bombastic and less liberal than the tenth itself. When they go to the polls to elect their own local officials — a village council, one of whose members is mayor, a local school board, and the park district board of trustees — Skokie's citizens tend to elect white professional men who are cautious if not conservative. The council, in turn, relies on the services of a salaried city manager and a lawyer on permanent retainer to the village; the result is a quietly efficient local government which seems to serve its constituency well most of the time.

Frank Collin's letter to Skokie went to the park district trustees (not to the village council) because Collins was seeking permission to stage a rally in one of Skokie's parks. Collin had written to a number of suburbs, but within a matter of days it was Skokie that had captured both his attention and his imagination.

While other suburbs either ignored Frank Collin's request or at least delayed before offering a vague denial, Skokie's park officials convened, took specific action in response to the request, and then quickly informed Collin of that action. Neighboring Evanston, for example, never replied to the letter Collin sent to them. Skokie, in perfect contrast, fired off a response.

Although the mere existence of a reply from Skokie set Skokie apart, it was the content of that reply which directly and inevitably drew Frank Collin to Skokie. The Board of Trustees of the Skokie Park District informed Frank Collin that he would have to provide bond or insurance in the amount of three hundred and fifty thousand dollars before he could be issued a permit to demonstrate in any of Skokie's parks.

Assuming the park district trustees did not want Frank Collin to come to Skokie, it is difficult — if not impossible — to imagine a more rashly inappropriate and ignorant action. There was no insurance requirement in Skokie's parks before Frank Collin wrote to the trustees. For that matter, the requirement was not enforced once Collin lost interest in Skokie's parks. The park district trustees actually created the requirement expressly for Frank Collin. Skokie's park officials did not simply pick a lousy weapon to use against Frank Collin by accident, they manufactured the weapon on purpose. In order to do that, the Skokie Park District officials either had to ignore, or fail to get, any sound advice.

If the trustees of the parks in Skokie did receive any legal advice on the matter, for example, they clearly ignored it. Any lawyer consulted about the Skokie insurance requirement would have found, at the minimum, several excellent reasons to select any other course than the one the trustees had picked.

On the first reading, the trustees' scheme was full of flaws that served to defeat their own goal of making Skokie's parks available to Skokie's citizens. An attorney would surely have noted the obvious fact that the trustees' insurance scheme would make it possible, on the one hand, for a rich Facist to parade through Skokie's parks while, on the other, precluding a less wealthy Republican candidate from doing exactly the same thing. By establishing price as the determining factor, the trustees censored the poor when, presumably, they wanted to censor the offensive. The insurance scheme also managed to preclude from the parks of Skokie all sorts of inoffensive groups who would, assuming equal application of the requirement, not be able to find the insurance. Thus, the Skokie trustees were adopting a plan to stop a Nazi demonstration that did not stop all Nazi demonstrations and that seemed to have the power to stop a group of Democrats bent on staging a picnic.

In addition, the insurance scheme managed to deprive the trustees of a major portion of control over their own parks. By leaving to bondsmen or insurance executives the decision of who would or would not be a good risk, Skokie's park district trustees effectively gave up their mandated right to make that same choice. Once an insurance company told a would-be demonstrator that the policy could be written, Skokie's park officials would have no more options.

All of those flaws, as major as they are, would have been apparent merely from a cursory examination of the requirement itself. A check on the state of the law, and presumably Skokie's officials would want to know if their action would violate the law, would have revealed flaws in the insurance scheme generally and in its application against Collin in particular.

An attorney checking on the law governing assemblies and insurance would have found *Collin* v. *O'Malley,* the suit in Chicago challenging the Chicago Park District insurance requirement. That discovery would have led, in turn, to a full examination of the legal flaws in such insurance plans, flaws carefully detailed in the papers filed with the court and available to everyone. Whatever legal issues the discovery might have raised would pale into insignificance next to the one unmistakable fact: the same name which appeared on the Chicago litigation appeared at the bottom of the letter Skokie's trustees had received.

That discovery, of course, would have almost certainly marked the end of any further consideration of the plan. To pass and then implement an insurance requirement specifically against an individual who was challenging in court exactly that requirement would be, at the very least, something of a taunt. At the most, it would seem a pure insult, particularly if (as Skokie park officials contemplated) the price was even higher than the one Collin had challenged in Chicago. Whatever else the Chicago litigation might have offered, it surely would have offered to Skokie's park officials proof positive that Frank Collin would react directly to an insurance requirement.

Yet Skokie's officials adopted such a requirement and rushed information about it to Frank Collin. Perhaps the village park officials hoped that Collin would sue Skokie, just as he had Chicago, and would thus tie himself up in litigation as he had in Chicago. Such a plan, if it actually existed in the minds of the trustees, would have been so thoroughly bankrupt that common sense alone would have caused its rejection.

Frank Collin can sue only if he can find an attorney. Collin's criminal counsel is usually court-appointed, but there is not a similar system of court appointment for civil matters (such as challenges to insurance requirements). Since the ACLU already had one suit on the matter of insurance schemes, it ought to have occurred to Skokie's officials that a second ACLU suit would serve no purpose; thus Collin, without ACLU's help, simply could not sue. Even more obvious was the fact that Collin had written to Skokie because he wanted to avoid litigation, not to generate more of it. In short, had they checked to find out something about the man whose name appeared before them in two different yet related contexts, Skokie's officials would have discovered that Frank Collin had no intention whatsoever of suing Skokie or any other locality.

In any event, it seems most unlikely that Skokie's officials had such a plan in mind. Such a plan would have required, very early on, the careful guidance of an attorney, an attorney who in all likelihood would have argued against the entire plan as both illegal and without any real short- or long-term benefit.

The most likely explanation for the actions of the park district trustees is also the most obvious: the trustees got a letter from a Nazi and, as quickly as they could, moved to stop him from coming to their parks with any weapon they could invent. They did not know who the Nazi was or what he represented or even what his strength might be, but they did know that his letter came with a black swastika and that was enough. The action they took was, ultimately, less rash than it was blind.

When he received the reply from the Skokie Park District, Collin instantly recognized his next target: Skokie had provided him with the perfect issue, a golden opportunity, all in a "predominantly Jewish" community. Collin had not singled out any community for attention when he first wrote letters to various suburbs. The park district reply provided Collin with the key he had sought, and as quickly as he could Collin began to turn it.

Frank Collin wrote back to the Village of Skokie. Instead of communicating further with the park district trustees, Collin now wrote to the village council. He informed the council that he and up to fifty followers would assemble on the sidewalk in front of the Skokie Village Hall for one-half hour on Sunday, May 1, 1977. The assembly would be confined to the sidewalk and the demonstrators would be in Neo-Nazi uniform, with swastikas on display, but no speeches would be given. Collin informed the village council that the purpose of the assembly was to protest the high insurance bond imposed on political assemblies by the Skokie Park District.

Frank Collin's plan was perfectly lawful, even if it seemed to give new meaning to the word by wedding an awful scheme to the law. Every citizen has the absolute right to disagree with the actions of government and every citizen has the right, within legal limits, to make that disagreement public. Frank Collin knew, better than most, the limits of his right to protest and the requirements of the law governing that right. His plan so perfectly combined both that even the Skokie Village Council and its lawyer recognized the legality of that plan.

Skokie's village council did not duplicate the mistakes of the park district trustees. Under the leadership of Mayor Albert Smith and the practical, wise guidance of Harvey Schwartz, the village's attorney, the Skokie Village Council responded to Frank Collin with all the tools the trustees had failed to employ, including common sense, a healthy respect for the law, and an overriding concern for the people of Skokie.

The council's response to Frank Collin rested, simply, on obedience to the law. Skokie would obey the law by permitting Collin his demonstration; since the law governing free speech and assembly allows for the airing of all points of view, those who opposed Collin would also be permitted to demonstrate. Collin, in turn, would be required to obey the law as well, confining his activity to legal protest and nothing more; so too would the counter-demonstrators be expected to confine their activities within lawful requirements.

From that basic principle, Skokie's council drew enormous advantage. By honoring the right to demonstrate, Skokie's officials gained control over the time, place, and manner of the demonstration itself; thus, the village officials could control the crowds by using the clock or by permitting demonstrations only in well-separated locations. The enormous power which such control afforded the council was in no way inconsistent with the rights of the demonstrators. Since the First Amendment is limited to guaranteeing the expression of all points of view, Skokie was only obligated to see that all ideas were aired, not that all ideas enjoyed an audience or exclusive access to a particular location.

The council, through the exercise of its powers to control the action, also became the recipient of all plans for the action. They already knew what Collin was planning to do, of course, and as quickly as his opposition decided to mobilize the council would know that, too. The advance knowledge the council gained through its control over the village's streets was an advantage in itself, since it afforded them the luxury of advance planning for police allocations, traffic patterns, and even hospital access routes.

33

The council's plan also recognized, and planned for, the obvious: if a Neo-Nazi came to Skokie, the people of the village would be sure to respond. By honoring the right to respond, Skokie's officials found the most secure and responsible way to let that reaction take place. A large counterdemonstration would serve the dual purpose of making it known that Skokie did not support Collin while allowing the villagers themselves to blow off the emotional steam built up by the mere presence of a Nazi in their hometown.

Above all else, however, Skokie's council attended to the law because if the law worked, Collin could come and go without significant turmoil or trouble. Above all else, the council wanted to show Collin that his presence would *not* hurt Skokie, for if he found the village truly vulnerable, he would surely never let go. By urging a calm, sensible response to Collin, Skokie's leaders hoped to prove to him that he had little to gain in their community. If he generated no real attention, or if at best he only caused a quiet, determined rejection, Collin would presumably find some other place in which to get attention.

Skokie's council elected to emphasize a calm and reasoned response to Collin by spreading the word of their plan through the clergy of the village. Albert Smith, Harvey Schwartz, and others met with representatives of all of the congregations in the village, urging each in turn to prevail upon their congregants for a restrained reaction to Collin's pending demonstration. With just less than a month remaining prior to the demonstration, Skokie's ministers, priests, and rabbis began to tell their congregations about the Nazi, his planned demonstration, the council's response to his plan, and the need for calm and restraint.

The village council's plan collapsed in the synagogues of Skokie. In each Jewish congregation before which the plan was presented, at least one member of the congregation expressed bitter, determined opposition to the whole scheme. Invariably, the criticism would come first from a holocaust survivor or a close relative of a survivor, and invariably the message would be the same: no matter the law, no matter the particulars about Frank Collin, no form of nazism should be allowed to raise a voice under any circumstances whatsoever. Although the actual words may never have been spoken in any of Skokie's seven synagogues, the message which was delivered was nevertheless unmistakable: Never Again!

As soon as the synagogue congregations heard survivors oppose the council's plan, the plan was doomed. The survivors' sole argument against allowing Collin a forum was the history that the survivors themselves represent. A challenge to the survivors' position thus became either a denial of history or an offer to repeat that history — such a challenge is virtual heresy in a synagogue. The strength of the survivors' position within the larger Jewish population was such that anyone who argued against it instantly became the object of wrath.

Not even the well-respected Anti-Defamation League could hold an audience of Jews in Skokie long enough to voice its position on the matter. The ADL — America's most respected enemy of anti-Semitism and the nation's best monitor of Neo-Nazism as well — was often called into synagogue meetings about the village council plan, usually as a resource for questions about the law and Collin. The ADL's official position was that Collin should not be censored but ignored. ADL representatives argued that Collin — weak and posing no threat — could gain only if he could cause turmoil; censorship would not work, the ADL argued, but shunning Collin would. In each instance, that position drew harsh, militant, angry opposition, and ADL representatives became enemies in the synagogues of Skokie.

With opposition so firmly set within the synagogues, the council's plan simply could not work. The larger community would surely look to Skokie's Jews for leadership on questions of nazism, and the Jewish community was not prepared to support the council's scheme.

While the weight of the survivor-generated opposition alone would surely have caused the collapse of the council's plan, other pressures quickly emerged which further undermined the plan. Rumors that made Collin seem still larger spread through the village, and the potential for violence became ever more real.

The rumors spread in spite of the efforts of the Anti-Defamation League. Perhaps because their position on the issue of Collin's right to march was so thoroughly rejected, the ADL's factual analysis of Collin was also ignored. At the same time, a group known as Concerned Jewish Citizens came forward to represent Jews opposed to the council's plan, and with CJC came rumors far more dramatic and inflammatory than anything the ADL could counter.

One of CJC's leaders was a woman named Erma Gans. A resident of Skokie, Ms. Gans is a survivor of the holocaust. She relied on a combination of two arguments to appeal to synagogue audiences: as a survivor, she argued persuasively against anything remotely resembling a repeat of the German horror; as an opponent of Frank Collin, she offered up sheer fantasy. Erma Gans consistently overestimated Collin's strength. She did not hesitate to suggest that Collin enjoyed "wealthy North Shore" financial support, and she painted Collin so broadly that he became almost indistinguishable from Hitler. Moreover, she defended her charges against Collin with exactly the same vehemence she brought to her moral arguments. In the same way that the compelling argument of the survivors worked against the Anti-Defamation League, it worked in favor of Erma Gans — so long as she said that Collin was a serious threat, no challenge to that view would be accepted by a Jewish audience.

The rumors served to solidify Jewish opposition to the council's plan, but it was ultimately the potential for violence which drove the council to abandon it. As the May 1 deadline grew closer, the signs of a violent reaction to Collin became so strong that the council could not ignore them.

From outside the village came flyers, produced by left-wing opponents to Collin and fascism. The flyers called upon all people to rally against Collin. They also gave an unmistakable warning to Skokie's council — there would be significant numbers of people from outside Skokie in the village on May 1, and the language of the flyers suggested that many would relish a physical confrontation with Frank Collin.

At the same time, another flyer circulating through the Village of Skokie raised the potential for a different source of violence. Frank Collin had produced a flyer announcing his arrival in Skokie, and it was eliciting an angry, violent response from the Jews of the village. Under the headline "Smash the Jewish System," Collin suggested that he was coming to Skokie because "where one finds the most Jews there one finds the most Jew-haters." The flyer, which displayed a crude and offensive caricature of a Jew and a swastika, frightened Skokie's Jews and dredged up in many an anger long forgotten.

The violent anger which Collin's flyer generated among some of Skokie's Jews was aroused among still others by a series of telephone calls. The calls, which came in the dead of night to Jewish residents of Skokie, were threatening in tone and anti-Semitic in content. The Skokie police could not determine the origin of the calls, but that did not matter to Skokie's Jews. As far as they were concerned, Frank Collin himself was placing those calls, and if he actually wanted to come to their village, an increasing number of Skokie's Jews were more than ready to talk back.

It was all too much for the village council — apart from the increasingly obvious threat to the security of the village which the council's plan seemed to guarantee, it was abundantly clear that the elected officials of the Village of Skokie were disregarding a vocal and important constituency. To serve their functions as protectors of the village and representatives of their constituents, the Skokie Village Council abandoned their plan.

On Wednesday, April 27, 1977, Harvey Schwartz — acting pursuant to a vote of the Skokie Village Council — filed suit against Frank Collin in the Circuit Court of Cook County. The Village of Skokie asked for an order from that court barring Frank Collin or the National Socialist Party of America from demonstrating, in uniform, in Skokie, Illinois, on May 1.

At about three o'clock on the afternoon of April 27, a process server delivered to Frank Collin notice of the

38

Village of Skokie's suit against him. Frank Collin read the document and reached for his telephone. He called the Illinois Division of the American Civil Liberties Union.

At the ACLU office in downtown Chicago the first — and only — warning about the explosive confrontation between Frank Collin, his Nazis, and the Village of Skokie came on the morning of April 27, 1977. While Skokie's lawyers were in a courtroom five blocks from the ACLU office pressing their suit to prevent Collin's scheduled demonstration, David Goldberger and I heard a rumor about that demonstration — and dismissed it.

David Goldberger heard the rumor first. He received a telephone call from a journalist and Illinois ACLU board member named Mike Hirsh who wanted to know if David could add anything to a rumor, circulating through the northern suburbs, about a "Nazi parade through Skokie." Goldberger, ACLU's legal director and the lawyer working on Collin's challenge to the Chicago Park District insurance requirement, had nothing to add. Goldberger's contact with Collin was limited almost exclusively to matters pertaining to the insurance litigation. David had a vague recollection that Collin had written to some suburbs, but he did not know to which suburbs or when, so there was nothing he could add to the rumor.

Within the hour, Goldberger passed the rumor along to me. While I sat in the remarkable clutter of his office having coffee, David told me about Hirsh's call and asked if I knew anything about the report. I had no contact of my own with Collin, and, while I had access to northern suburban press coverage which Goldberger (a south-sider) would not be likely to see, I had noticed nothing in my papers about Collin or Skokie. Between the two of us, we did not have enough information to talk about the rumor for more than a moment or two — and that was all we gave it.

The balance of our conversation on that morning was devoted to matters which David and I were confident held more import than unverified rumors. We discussed, among other things, an approaching special meeting of our board and our strategy for that meeting; we talked about several pending ACLU cases and an equal number of potential suits; we talked about several news and courtroom developments related to our work. We also talked about the Chicago Cubs and David's wife's work and my son's birthday — we had so naturally merged our friendship into our work that the two were all but inseparable.

David Goldberger and I had, essentially, hired each other for our respective ACLU positions. David had served on the board committee which had recommended my selection as executive director. He and a handful of others, including the president of the board, Frank Haiman, had lobbied hard for my selection. Within a year of my arrival in Chicago, I had hired David to his second stint as legal director.

David's first stint with ACLU began when he graduated from the University of Chicago's school of law. For the next several years, years which included the 1968 Democratic Convention and the litigation arising from it as well as some major civil-rights litigation, David learned litigation and civil liberties, eventually becoming the Illinois Division's legal director. When staff turmoil set in (as often happens in ACLU), the division went through two executive directors in all but that number of years, and David left to work for the local legal assistance group.

I had come to ACLU in 1970, assuming a position as the first (and only) full-time employee of the New Hampshire Civil Liberties Union. I spent four years there, learning everything from the considerable internal mechanics of ACLU to the value of civil liberties and the strategies for safeguarding them.

For an education in basic civil-liberties advocacy, New Hampshire was the ideal training ground. The state's infamous newspaper publisher William Loeb provided daily lessons in intolerance, contempt for basic rights, and inequality. When Loeb was not advocating the incarceration of anyone who exercised any First Amendment right other than the right to worship, he displayed remarkable bigotry — William Loeb once headlined a front-page editorial about the then secretary of state "Kissinger the Kike."

When William Loeb's candidate for governor, Meldrim Thomson, finally got elected, New Hampshire entered a new phase of limited democracy: Thomson attempted to all but revoke the citizenship of gay students in the state, treated women with open contempt, attempted to shut down a prisoner-support demonstration with a high bond (which ACLU lawyers knocked down), and occasionally engaged in vigilante law enforcement for the sport of it. For those of us who watched him, it came as no surprise when Thomson, some years later, asked the Pentagon to issue tactical nuclear weapons to his state's National Guard.

In that environment, my education in civil liberties was always stimulating and usually challenging. Each new Loeb-sided attack would require a response which I (having no law degree, a circumstance common to most ACLU directors) would have to fashion from ACLU's written policies and whatever quick advice I could get from volunteer attorneys. I also began to learn to work with the press and to develop a skill for responding to almost anything quickly and briefly, an essential talent for any electronic coverage. When I was in the public arena working with clearly defined issues, the work was thrilling.

ACLU left a lot to be desired as a continuing place of employment in spite of the rewards which the substantive work provided. For one thing, ACLU salaries are abysmal as the result of an inevitable set of priorities which place the "cause" above the employees. For another, ACLU's membership system, with which affiliate staff must work on a daily basis, was until very recently one of the most complicated and self-defeating such systems ever created by man.

Until it was finally overhauled (in the late 1970s), ACLU's membership system was a combination of error-ridden computer programs, a billing system which always confused and usually angered the entire membership, and a series of administrative decisions which seemed ever more incomprehensible.

Even without the in-house frustrations of such inefficiency, ACLU employment will always have high turnover rates. Most ACLU offices around the country have a single employee, who is responsible for the newsletters, press coverage, the screening and tracking of all cases, the care and feeding of the membership and the local board, the filing, the speaking, and the funding. In all but the biggest ACLU affiliates, the executive director answers the telephone and talks to whoever walks through the doors — and through ACLU doors will eventually pass every terrified paranoid, cheated victim, wronged weakling, and angry borderline crazy free to walk the streets. It can be lonely and very depressing work indeed.

Such considerations had led me, by the spring of 1974, to contemplate employment elsewhere. Before I could even solidify my feelings, however, Richard Nixon managed to offend Charles Morgan's sense of justice.

Charles Morgan was ACLU's chief lobbyist in Washington. He saw in Richard Nixon's various constitutional transgressions a chain of evidence leading directly to impeachment hearings. In his lyrically righteous overpowering style, Charles Morgan launched a crusade; with the zeal of a missionary, he set out to have ACLU become the first national organization to call for Nixon's impeachment.

The ACLU board of directors debate on impeachment, which occurred in June 1974, was probably a historic event. Certainly it is true that the board's decision at that meeting began the series of public events that would have led to Nixon's inevitable impeachment; the air of tension which attended that debate suggested that the board itself knew what was coming. When it was over — after every conceivable point of view had been thoroughly and carefully examined — the ACLU national board voted to actively pursue the impeachment of the President of the United States.

The effect of participation in such heady events can be positively intoxicating, sufficient to cause otherwise sensible people to work for low salaries under sometimes sour conditions — thus is the American Civil Liberties Union staffed from coast to coast. I found I was no exception. The opportunity to work within an organization capable of such momentous decisions and actions was virtually irresistible; within weeks of the impeachment vote, I had applied for two ACLU directorships in states with larger operations than New Hampshire's.

While the Michigan affiliate took a long, long time to hire a new director, the Illinois division (which is also an affiliate of ACLU, the "division" being mere pretense) had the system down to a fine art. Since they were hiring their third director in four years, the Illinois board was almost jaded about the entire process. Still, before the summer had ended I had been interviewed by the board's screening committee twice, by the Chicago ACLU staff once, and by the full fifty-odd-member board of directors as well.

I met David Goldberger during the first of those interviews. He had been seated on the Illinois board as soon as he had resigned his staff position; his staff experience in turn made him an obvious choice for the board's screening committee. Our alliance began when, in response to a question (seeking to determine why I wanted to work for ACLU if I could earn more elsewhere), I said I was having a "love affair with the First Amendment." In the back of the room, David Goldberger sat bolt upright in his chair and grinned when he heard that.

The Illinois board hired me. They viewed that decision as a high-risk proposition (and told me so in a long pre-employment memo), and I did my level best to justify that view for almost a year. The staff in Chicago had almost unanimously opposed my selection for one thing, so my arrival had all the amity of a Nixon press conference, and in the months that followed there was an inordinate amount of staff turnover. Because of my own inexperience and the almost overwhelming size of the Illinois operation (which was by comparison to New Hampshire absolutely monstrous), I committed a number of outrageous mistakes, the most critical of which, I still believe, ought to have led to my dismissal. Moreover, my wife and I had separated when I moved to Chicago, and our five-year-old son came to live with me within months of the move, so I was also learning about the challenges and demands of single parenthood.

Through most of that first long year, I had the considerable protection and guidance of an informal "kitchen cabinet." Composed of Board President Frank Haiman (in his twelfth term, and every bit as wise as he was powerful) and others from the board, the group included from the beginning David Goldberger. As a former staff member, a respected voice on the board, and a lawyer who viewed (with considerable justification) the entire legal structure of Chicago as his own private turf, Goldberger was among my most valuable allies.

When David Goldberger's successor as legal director resigned toward the end of my first year, it represented a significant turning point. Not only did the resignation rid the staff of the most vocal opponent to my selection, it afforded me the chance to fill the other senior staff position in the office with someone whose strengths could balance my more glaring weaknesses. So I did not hesitate to offer David Goldberger the job, and David barely hesitated before he accepted it.

By the time Frank Collin called about Skokie, David and I had worked together for nearly two years. We had discovered, in the first weeks of our working partnership, that we shared an uncommonly similar view of ACLU and our roles within it. We discovered as well that we shared our passion: David had laughed at my "love affair with the

First Amendment" out of empathy, not amusement, because his love for his work far exceeded mine. On the strength of those common bonds, we quickly established a trusting, respectful relationship, which was occasionally noisy but always harmonic.

In the months before Collin called, David and I and the rest of the ACLU staff had been working a rich field of issues other than Fascists' rights. David was in the midst of a brawl with the U.S. Immigration Service, an agency which seemed determined to arrest every human being in the Midwest who "looks Mexican." Lois Lipton, our staff counsel, managed her half of the ninety-odd-case docket (sharing that duty with David), while she also frustrated the state legislature's various annual attempts to escape, evade, or ignore the law of the land governing abortion rights. While I was supervising the rest of the staff (including fund-raisers, staff assistants, volunteers, and secretaries) and keeping the board fed and cared for, I tried as well to keep at least a finger or two on real civil-liberties issues. Among them, as Collin began his correspondence with Skokie, were police spying and the FBI's massive files on ACLU, which I had been trying to obtain through the Freedom of Information Act.

While all of that and more was occurring, David and I were also paying attention to Marquette Park and the likelihood of demonstrations and counterdemonstrations there as soon as the weather turned. The First Amendment considerations which were equally likely to arise were not far from our thoughts, in part because we knew about the insurance requirement and Collin's previous arrest in the park and in part because David — as ever — was taking his city's pulse. From what he learned through his many contacts (lawyers, politicians, ministers, police), David became increasingly more confident of the prospect of Marquette Park litigation.

To that end, in fact, David and I were engaged in a series of meetings with members of the Martin Luther King, Jr. Movement Coalition, the most prominent and active of the black groups opposed to Collin in and around Marquette Park. Since we knew that the city's response would be just as likely to stifle the coalition's rights as Collin's, we were engaged in discussions with the coalition about the circumstances under which ACLU might represent them. While those meetings were sometimes tense, for the coalition's representatives were understandably uneasy about accepting legal services from the same organization representing their enemy, the exchanges were open and frank. Among other things, it became unquestionably clear that if the coalition could get into the park to demonstrate, they would.

Because Goldberger and I both felt that the issues presented by the coming confrontations in the park were important enough to merit the attention of our board of directors, we entered on the board's April agenda a discussion of Marquette Park. We intended, under that general heading, to actually discuss several matters with the board. We wanted to bring the board up to date on our meetings with the King coalition and on the information we had gained from those meetings, but we also wanted to remind the board of our current participation in the controversies through the Collin insurance litigation. At the same time, David and I felt that a discussion in advance of a potentially controversial role would both solidify the board's First Amendment position and, perhaps, prepare the board for the tougher discussions that it might face later.

To accomplish all of that and focus the board's attention on the larger issues in Marquette Park, David suggested that we show the board a film — shot by Chicago Police Department technicians — of the demonstration that Collin had staged in Marquette Park the previous September. David had discovered the film during the course of the defense which ACLU had provided Collin, and he felt it would be an ideal tool with which to educate the board.

On Thursday, April 21, the board met at noon. After a bit of routine business, housekeeping chores, and lunch, David introduced the film. He explained that a summer's worth of demonstrations and tensions had led up to the incidents portrayed in the film and reminded the board that the arrest of Frank Collin they were going to witness had later been thrown out of court.

The movie — with sound — was exceptionally good. It accurately captured the tone and texture of the neighborhood with a long series of crowd shots taken from a moving truck, shots which featured black and white youths and adults roaming the streets and sidewalks of their neighborhood looking for action. The film captured the unmistakable signs and shouted slogans of racial tension and then shifted to a view of Frank Collin, in full Neo-Nazi uniform, surrounded by four or five uniformed followers.

The ACLU board greeted Frank Collin's image on the screen with a low murmur of anger. There were scattered snorts of disapproval, and one woman spat out a stage-whispered evaluation of the man on the screen ("Bastard!"), but those reactions and the nervous laughter which also greeted Collin were swallowed up in a sustained grumble of hardly concealed hostility. That undercurrent of anger was sustained in the debate which followed the film.

The ACLU board attempted — in the very short time it had remaining on that Thursday afternoon — to sort out the two starkly clashing facts portrayed in the film. On the one hand, Collin's nazism was clearly an abrasive, catalytic force in a community which needed nothing less than more racial hatred; yet, on the other hand, the arrest shown in the film was so flagrantly unconstitutional that even the most vehement of the board's anti-Fascist contingent could not defend it. As a body charged with setting policy aimed at fostering equality and protecting freedom of speech, the ACLU group in the room that afternoon was at odds with itself.

Before the dilemma could be solved, the board adjourned. Although some in the room argued that ACLU should at least reconsider its traditional position of First Amendment defense, no proposition to that effect was put to the board. Before adjourning, however, the board scheduled a special meeting for the first week of May to debate and resolve the Marquette Park policy problems.

Six days later Frank Collin called the ACLU office. In a fifteen-minute conversation, Collin outlined for Goldberger the basic events which had led to Skokie's lawsuit and read him the summons with which Collin had been served that morning. When the call was completed, Goldberger came to my office and outlined Skokie's case.

In the constitutional terms which we used to analyze the case that afternoon, it was a classic confrontation. The village of Skokie was attempting to censor, in advance of the actual activity, political demonstrating that was clearly under the protection of the First Amendment. It was Skokie's theory that the demonstration could be prevented because the audience — not Frank Collin — might break the law. David and I agreed that Skokie was seeking a form of prior restraint that is traditionally and strongly forbidden by American law. We did not need much time to decide that ACLU had to act to prevent the village from engaging in pure political censorship.

We understood that our decision put us in something of a conflict with our own board of directors. Although they had reserved decision on the narrow question of future participation in Marquette Park litigation, the board had obviously done so out of a hesitancy to represent Frank Collin. The board felt strongly enough about the problem to schedule an extra meeting, and before that meeting could take place (but after the board's reservations had been well aired) the staff put Collin on the docket. Neither David nor I felt we could take such an action on our own authority, so we called the president of ACLU's board.

Edwin Rothschild had been an ACLU board member for a long time and a lawyer dedicated to ACLU's work for even longer. Although he is a senior partner in a massive Chicago law firm, Rothschild never failed to have time for his friends on the staff at ACLU and always gave us more than we asked. In this instance, Rothschild listened as David outlined the Skokie case and then listened some more as David and I outlined our position. When he was satisfied that he had all the facts he needed, Edwin Rothschild ordered his staff to place the Skokie litigation on the ACLU docket.

The "order" was designed, I am confident, to protect

50

the staff. Rothschild, who was as sensitive as David and I were to the lines of responsibility and authority in our organization, simply moved to deflect the heat of the decision higher up on the ladder, toward himself and away from us. Rothschild's solution to the political problem was also the ideal posture for ACLU as well, for if we were to take on what could be controversial litigation, we would have to do so from strength. Rothschild's solution temporarily resolved the possible staff and board conflict. It also created a consensus among the three principal officers of the organization. Satisfied that there was nothing more he could do to help, Edwin repeated his order (lest there be any misunderstanding) and rang off wishing us good luck.

It was, by then, late in the afternoon. Skokie's case against Collin's demonstration was scheduled for a hearing the following morning, so time had become a critical factor. If there was going to be any significant preparation for the court hearing in the morning, somebody was going to have to work that evening. David spent the remainder of the afternoon trying to find a volunteer attorney to take the litigation. Most ACLU cases are handled in part or in whole by volunteers, although a few are litigated exclusively by staff counsel. The few lawyers who could be reached could not alter their own court schedules quickly enough to accommodate David's request even if they had wanted to, which they probably didn't. When the working day ended, David had decided that he would have to take the case himself.

Goldberger stopped by my office to tell me of his decision and to inform me that he had spoken with Barbara O'Toole. Barbara is an attorney and a long-time friend of David who had volunteered for ACLU cases on a very selective basis for years after a brief turn as a staff attorney; she and David shared so much litigation together that she had an office within ACLU's offices. Not surprisingly, then, Barbara had agreed to help with the preparation of the Skokie case, although David would do all arguing in court. I agreed that I would handle whatever press coverage occurred at the hearing itself and in the aftermath of the hearing as well, our theory being that David would be thus freed to devote his time to the litigation itself.

In the quiet moments as the office began to empty at the end of the day, David and I talked briefly about the Skokie case. We talked about the content of the case, about what we might expect from the court in the morning, about the general arguments David expected to put before the court. We did not talk about a broad public reaction to the case or to our efforts in it, because we did not expect such a reaction.

On the morning of April 28, 1977, Frank Collin and his National Socialist Party of America, the Village of Skokie, and the Illinois Division of the American Civil Liberties Union were drawn into a courtroom in the Richard J. Daley Civic Center in downtown Chicago. Within hours, all hell would break loose.

3

"A Classic First Amendment Case"

On the morning of April 28, five minutes after Cook County Chancery Judge Joseph Wosik had called to order the hearing of *Village of Skokie* v. *Collin,* David Goldberger rose to address the court:

"This is a classic First Admendment case, your Honor. It tests the very foundations of democracy. The Village of Skokie moves for an order enjoining speech before it has occurred even though that speech is to occur in an orderly fashion in front of the Village Hall for a period of between twenty and thirty minutes on a Sunday afternoon, this Sunday afternoon. Such an order, whatever we might feel about the content of the speech, violates the very essence of the First Amendment."

Goldberger had correctly outlined the facts in the case, and he had properly delineated the law governing those facts as well, but neither facts nor law would make very much difference in Judge Wosik's courtroom that day. The very essence of the First Admendment was about to be subordinated to such considerations as politics, prejudice, and more than a hint of impropriety.

The political considerations which pressured Judge Wosik were reasonably obvious even before the case had been called to order. Before Wosik was a case in which he had two clear options: he could rule in favor of Collin and thus unleash on an attractive and beleaguered suburb a band of hate-mongers whose particular venom would sting the residents of that suburb most painfully, or he could rule in favor of Skokie and strike a blow against bigotry while protecting a community from the ravages of nazism. Since Judge Joseph Wosik is elected, his options were hardly difficult to assess with or without the facts and the law.

In any event, Judge Joseph Wosik barely had enough time to identify his options before most of those options were removed from his consideration by an unusual — and almost certainly improper — telephone call from a highly placed member of the Cook County Regular Democratic Organization.

The telephone call came very early in the proceedings, before Skokie's case was on the record and before Collin's defense had been presented. While the lawyers for both sides were still engaged in preliminary fencing, Judge Wosik's secretary poked her head into the courtroom to inform the judge (and all of us present in the room at the time) that Cook County Sheriff Richard Elrod was waiting for the judge on the judge's office telephone. Judge Wosik recessed his hearing, rose from his bench, and left the court to take his call.

There is no record of the telephone call. The lawyers for both sides remained in the court along with the recorder assigned to the courtroom. Since there is no record of the call, there is nothing to prove that the sheriff and the judge talked about the Skokie case — nothing except the fact that Sheriff Elrod had an indisputable interest in the outcome of the case and the fact that, when Wosik returned to the courtroom, he was full of misinformation about, and barely concealed anger with, Frank Collin's recent activities in Marquette Park.

It is possible that Sheriff Elrod simply wanted to talk with Judge Wosik about security. Turmoil does, after all, accompany personalities such as Collin's, and it is conceivable that Elrod wanted to be sure that the courtroom was safe and sound. To do so, of course, he would logically call his own men in the building, not the judge sitting on the case at that moment. Since the security which was already in place when Collin arrived in the courtroom was obviously adequate, there was little need for Elrod's intervention in that particular matter anyhow.

Almost certainly, Sheriff Elrod's intervention in the matter before Judge Wosik had more to do with the safety of Skokie itself than with the security of the courthouse. Sheriff Richard Elrod, without question, had responsibilities which tied him directly to the potential demonstration in Skokie. If Skokie's police department needed back-up manpower, one of the first to be called would be Elrod, whose deputies often serve as such reserve personnel. If Skokie called several nearby suburbs for additional policemen, Elrod's office would be more than likely to provide assistance and coordination. In short, Sheriff Richard Elrod was in the position of a Skokie law enforcement official, once removed. When he spoke with Judge Wosik, his concerns were almost precisely the same as those of the lawyers representing the village in the courtroom.

Thus, Richard Elrod was a potential, if not actual, party to the litigation before Judge Wosik. That fact alone would have made the hearing which followed suspect in most judicial jurisdictions, but that fact was hardly alone in this instance. After the telephone call, Judge Wosik exhibited a bias against Frank Collin so substantial that Wosik could hardly wait to attack him.

At the first opportunity Judge Wosik began to lecture Frank Collin on his activities in Marquette Park. Wosik's comments were out of place, out of context, and markedly out of touch with the facts, but none of that mattered as much as the fact that Wosik clearly wanted to let Collin know how he felt.

Skokie's lawyers had not alluded to Collin's past activities when Wosik's lecture to Collin began, so the judge was not simply following a line of argument raised by one of the opposing sides in the case; he was raising an argument of his own. Moreover, since there was no legal relationship whatsoever between Marquette Park and Skokie, the judge's comments were all but improper, since they suggested that Wosik had information about Collin which clearly clouded the judge's judgment.

The information the judge used was, moreover, almost entirely wrong. Judge Wosik attributed to Collin and his organization a rally which had resulted in injuries, but that rally had in fact been organized and carried out by the Martin Luther King, Jr. Movement Coalition. In addition, Wosik managed to confuse a previous case against Collin with the rally staged by the King group, a confusion which both reinforced Wosik's obvious bias and distorted beyond redemption the facts of the matter.

Richard Elrod, of course, was never in the courtroom. Thus, to note but one of the potential miscarriages of justice which Wosik's actions suggested, neither Skokie's lawyers nor Collin's had any chance to examine or cross-examine Elrod's statements. If the sheriff had provided

Judge Wosik with misinformation, there was no effective way to correct it; if Elrod had somehow influenced Judge Wosik's view of Collin and Collin's demonstration plans, there was no way to erase the bias.

In the rest of the nation, such potentially unjust actions might lead to careful scrutiny of the judge's behavior. In the lower reaches of the Illinois judicial system, however, there is very little relationship between justice and judges, and the rules of evidence have been borrowed from *Alice in Wonderland* ("Sentencing first," ordered the Red Queen, "trial afterward"); so Judge Wosik was simply engaged in business as usual. Once the telephone call and its aftermath had run their course, the only unfinished business before Judge Wosik was the presentation of Skokie's case.

The case which Skokie presented to Judge Wosik rested exclusively on a single, subtle twist of legal logic: if Frank Collin is permitted to demonstrate in the Village of Skokie, residents of the village will almost certainly break the law; therefore, Frank Collin must not be permitted to demonstrate. Although the broad public debate which grew around Skokie's position came to include virtually all aspects of First Amendment law, the case which represented Skokie's primary legal line of defense against Frank Collin lay entirely with the theory known as the "heckler's veto."

The heckler's veto takes its name from the wonderfully passionate scholarship of a University of Chicago professor of law, the late Harry Kalven. Kalven's work — which explores and examines the theory completely — anticipated Skokie's dilemma almost perfectly. Skokie could not argue that Collin himself would break the law, for there was nothing illegal in Collin's proposed demonstration; yet Skokie was convinced that, if Collin appeared, the law would nevertheless be broken. Thus, as Kalven foresaw, Skokie argued that the audience's reaction to the speaker could be grounds for censoring the speaker. Although Kalven taught his students that the theory is flatly unconstitutional, it was nevertheless Skokie's best weapon.

Skokie's heavy reliance on the heckler's veto grew out of the very subtlety of the theory itself. What Skokie wanted most to do was the one thing which two hundred years of American political tradition and law flatly forbid — Skokie wanted most of all to censor an idea based on the content of that idea. Instead, Skokie adopted a theory which is, in effect, pure censorship once removed — by arguing that the audience's reaction to the idea would be illegal, Skokie arrived at the closest possible position to the one they wanted most to argue.

In order to establish the foundation for the theory, Skokie used five witnesses. They included the mayor of the village, a holocaust survivor residing in the village, a leader of the organized Jewish community in Skokie, a resident of the village who had obtained a copy of the flyer distributed by Collin's organization announcing the demonstration, and (last but absolutely not least) Frank Collin himself.

The resident who had a copy of Collin's flyer was, for all intents and purposes, incidental to the proceedings. He simply articulated for the court the circumstances under which he had come to have a copy of the flyer. It was, in fact, the flyer itself which Skokie's lawyers wanted on the witness stand.

The flyer, crudely done, was a double-sided sheet of standard-sized paper. On one side, amid phrases such as "where one finds the most Jews, there one will find the most Jew-haters," the demonstration itself was announced — time, place, date, and so forth. On the other side was a crude cartoon, depicting a massive swastika and an offensive caricature of a Jewish man under the large words "Smash the Jew System."

Once the paper was in evidence, Skokie's lawyers used it time and again to drive home the only point they wanted to make: the audience would more than likely react violently to this demonstration. If Collin was as offensive as his flyer, the villagers would surely erupt.

Each of Skokie's other witnesses drove home the same point. Fred Richter, the leader of the organized Jewish community within the village, described the turmoil which gripped every synagogue in the community, and he characterized the potential for violence from those congregants as quite real. Similarly, the mayor of the village, Albert Smith, testified angrily about the high emotion and fear which gripped a substantial portion of his community.

At the very heart of Skokie's argument lay an obvious, but ultimately useless, fact: the residents of the village of Skokie are uniquely vulnerable to the hatred which Collin spews. To make that point unmistakably clear, the village called to the witness stand Sol Goldstein, a holocaust survivor who lives in the village.

The village's lawyers could not have selected a better witness. In Sol Goldstein, they had the fierce anger of their community personified. When Goldstein took the witness

59

stand, he found himself face to face, across an expanse of perhaps eight feet, with Frank Collin. Goldstein fixed Collin with a stare which literally made Collin squirm — and held that glare throughout his testimony.

Sol Goldstein, who had himself fought in the resistance against facism, described in harsh detail the ordeal of his survival — the deaths of his close family at the hands of barbaric human beings, the agony of his memories. When Skokie's lawyer asked Goldstein if he would attack Frank Collin should Collin appear in the village, Goldstein, still staring at Collin, replied very softly, "I may . . ." The ambiguity of the answer did not fool a soul in the room.

To bring their argument full circle — to prove that the audience's reaction to Collin was both predictable and justified — Skokie used Frank Collin himself as their star, if hostile, witness. To convince the court that Collin would certainly draw a very hostile reaction, Skokie sought to place on the record everything they could about Frank Collin's political beliefs.

Gilbert Gordon, working as Harvey Schwartz's co-counsel in the case on behalf of the village, handed Frank Collin a copy of his own flyer. When Collin had examined the document quickly, Gordon asked him if he agreed with the contents.

David Goldberger objected instantly: "His personal views are irrelevant here. . . . Our theory of the case, your Honor, is that neither the court nor the Village of Skokie ought to be able to select speakers based on their views."

The court overruled.

Gordon asked Frank Collin if Collin had read, and agreed with, *Mein Kampf*. Goldberger again rose to object. ". . . it is the theory of the United States Constitution that a man is on trial, not for his ideas — ever — but for what he intends to do . . . or what he does."

The court again overruled. So it went, until Skokie had managed to place Frank Collin's political point of view on the record. The case was complete once Collin had testified for Skokie — by first establishing the probability of a violent audience reaction and by then purporting to establish the reasons for that reaction, Skokie had managed to put the idea on trial after all.

The case which David Goldberger presented to the court was as simple — if somewhat less subtle — as Skokie's. There had been no allegation by Skokie's lawyers at any time during the presentation of their case that Frank Collin intended to break the law. Because there was no evidence of unlawful intent, the court was powerless to act, for unless the law will be broken and that fact can be proved beyond doubt, courts are simply not allowed to stop speech before it takes place.

Goldberger put Collin on the stand again. This time, Collin went briefly over the events which had led to the proposed demonstration and recited once more the plan for that demonstration. He told the court that the demonstration would last less than an hour, that the marchers would carry signs proclaiming "Free Speech for Whites" and similar slogans (none, Collin indicated, of an anti-Semitic nature), and that there would be no speeches given and no literature distributed. Skokie passed its opportunity to cross-examine Frank Collin when he had completed his recitation for Judge Wosik, so there the matter rested. David Goldberger argued, once again, that without any showing of illegal intent the court simply could not act to prevent Collin's constitutionally protected demonstration.

Judge Wosik, of course, viewed the law in quite a different way. Before he had heard a word from Skokie's witnesses, Wosik had indicated his tentative conviction that Frank Collin generates violence; with very deft guidance from the village's lawyers, Skokie's witnesses had substantially reinforced that conviction. When David Goldberger rested for the defense, Judge Wosik paused for a moment or two and then issued his order.

The order was an injunction, issued against Frank Collin and the National Socialist Party of America. Collin and his organization were banned from parading in uniform in the village of Skokie on May 1, 1977.

Judge Wosik adjourned the hearing and left his courtroom. The Skokie witnesses and their friends and supporters moved quickly to one counsel table, as I joined David and a handful of reporters at the other. David and I told the reporters that we fully expected to appeal Judge Wosik's order and did our best to explain our presence in the case and our theory of it. The reporters also got quick statements from Harvey Schwartz and Albert Smith, as David and I left the courtroom.

There was one television crew waiting in the hall. The reporter snared David, setting him up in the circle of portable lights, and David repeated his statements once more. The reporter then moved Frank Collin into the circle, which by now included a group of onlookers as well as lights.

Collin, in his nasal, smug tone, spoke about his plans for the demonstration and about his rights. Although he took no pains to hide his basic philosophy, Collin did not say anything overtly anti-Semitic; Collin also told the reporter

that he would not violate the court's order. In the middle
of the interview, one of the bystanders began to shout,
first at Collin ("You bastard!") and then at the reporter
for letting Collin have the camera. The man waved his fist
wildly in the general direction of Frank Collin as the
camera turned to catch him, but the incident went no
further. David and I left the building.

As we walked back to ACLU's office, David, Barbara
O'Toole, and I shared our reactions to the morning's
events. I expressed my amazement at the telephone call,
while Barbara leveled a series of sarcastic shots at the
dramatic way in which Skokie's lawyer, Gil Gordon,
had played his role. Goldberger, both shocked and angry,
demanded to know how Judge Wosik could agree that
lawlessness in Skokie was inevitable without hearing a
word from the people charged with maintaining the law —
Skokie's police. The village's evidence had not included a
single word from the local law enforcement officials, so
Wosik had absolutely no way of determining whether or
not they believed they could do their job. Yet if the
police in Skokie were competent, lawlessness was not
inevitable.

We agreed that such a lapse could occur only in a state
court. Litigation involving civil liberties guaranteed by
the U.S. Constitution arises mainly in the federal court
system, and all legal questions involving those rights are
inevitably resolved by the federal system. State courts thus
have limited direct experience with such matters. A federal
judge would almost certainly have dismissed Skokie's case
in the absence of some proof of inevitable illegal activity,
whereas Judge Wosik did not even bother to search for

that proof. We understood, without saying so, that by filing their case in the state system Skokie's lawyers had taken a significant "home court" advantage in the litigation.

Our analysis of the hearing ended when we reached our office. It had taken about twenty minutes to walk from Judge Wosik's court to ACLU's office; in that time, the first news accounts of the Skokie controversy had reached the public, and all hell had broken loose.

The office was alive with tension. The calls of protest were coming into our telephone system so rapidly that the system could not carry all of the calls. Between reporters who had to have details and quotes and citizens who had to let us know how they felt, the telephones all but broke under the load.

I took the calls while David prepared the appeal. For the balance of that day — and for hours every day for the next two weeks — I talked with people who could not contain their anger at ACLU's action.

The calls quickly fell into a pattern. Nobody called to express their support of ACLU's position; the only calls which did not protest our work were those from reporters. Virtually all of the callers identified themselves as Jewish, and a substantial majority of all the calls went beyond the issues of the controversy itself into territory that was at once surprising and shocking.

Among the very first of the calls I answered, for example, was one from an exceedingly angry woman. She argued with ACLU's legal position for a while, until she realized that I was not going to alter my view of our role in the matter; when her arguments failed, the woman asked her first, and only, question.

"Young man," the woman asked, "are you Jewish?"

It did not occur to me to refuse to answer — I am not Jewish.

"My God," whispered the woman, "I *spit* on you!"

Before the day had ended I had come to view the woman's call as one of the more moderate — and more pleasant — protests.

A man who identified himself as a lawyer suggested that only the son of parents who had served as guards in Hitler's camps could take the position I argued.

An elderly man asked a number of sensible questions about the controversy; when he did not care for the answers he got, he offered to torture members of my family so that I could fully appreciate the issue.

A substantial number of the callers assumed that both David and I were Fascists; a still larger number expressed the idea that our support of Collin ran to his platform as well as his right to demonstrate.

Several callers made direct threats against my life or David's; a woman with a very soft voice told me she was going to buy a bomb and mail it to us.

A youngster called, and, while his father shouted encouragement in the background, unleashed a string of obscenities, which included several untoward references to my lineage.

A few callers, armed with the knowledge that Goldberger is Jewish, accused me of seducing him into the case; one woman insisted that I remain quiet while she talked, lest I confuse her the way I had confused David.

The anger which ran through most of the calls was more than sufficient to create an air of siege in the office, but the anger was not the most common element in the calls.

The single most common factor among the calls was also the most astonishing: nobody knew the facts of the dispute. While hundreds of people called ACLU to protest our actions in the case, not one of them knew the basic facts in that case.

The pervasive misinformation about the Skokie controversy was the product of Chicago's journalistic community. The enormous competitive strain in that community governs all of the work it does. Chicago is the third largest media market in the nation, so it offers to the successful purveyor of news profits which are measured in the millions of dollars. At the same time, however, Chicago has none of the population padding of either New York or Los Angeles, so it offers to a marginal news operation only failure.

The result of that demographic fact is severe competition in which losers are left bleeding for all to see. The Chicago *Daily News*, the city's last major daily afternoon newspaper, lost its battle with early evening television news broadcasts, and the price of losing was hardly gentle: the paper simply died, putting reporters, pressmen, and hundreds of others out of work. While the *Daily News* was engaged in its death struggle, one of the three network-owned television stations lost its very popular anchorman, and with him went ratings and all of those millions in profit. The station proceeded to chew up and spit out several replacements in the space of months.

When the stakes are that high and the room for failure is almost nonexistent, the inevitable result is a do-or-die mentality, which suffuses every aspect of journalism in Chicago. The drive to be "number one" in the market is paramount; the race to be "first" is what makes journalism tick in the city.

The earliest reports of the Skokie controversy displayed the best and the worst of that competition. Several reporters managed to get their stories out to the public within minutes of Judge Wosik's ruling, thus unquestionably satisfying their editors' urgings to be "first." At the same time, of course, the rush to file the stories led to something less than completely accurate reporting, and the errors which were generated in those first reports lasted throughout the duration of the controversy.

Several early reports of the dispute (and countless reports thereafter) used as interchangeable the prepositions "in" and "through" to describe Frank Collin's proposed demonstration. Thus, a substantial number of people heard that Frank Collin planned to "march through Skokie." Since speed was the premium commodity, little if any further explanation of the plan was offered, leaving the most essential details to the imaginations of the listeners.

As a direct consequence of that prepositional inaccuracy, a huge number of people believed that Collin would, in fact, march "through Skokie." Since the reports also indicated that Skokie is populated in large numbers by Jews, those who heard "through" quite naturally assumed that any march "through" the village would have to pass the homes of Jewish residents. Those who did not assume the residential march at least assumed that Collin would pass synagogues in the village.

The hasty reports also failed to describe Collin's proposed activity beyond two-word definitions: "Nazi

67

parade," "Neo-Nazi demonstration," "Nazi rally." Those shorthand descriptions, while certainly not entirely inaccurate, nevertheless left out a good deal of factual data. Lacking information to the contrary, most people assumed that Collin's "rally" would be like other rallies they knew about and that meant speeches; since everyone knew about Collin's philosophy, most assumed the speeches would be anti-Semitic.

So those who called ACLU to protest did so with high emotion and low understanding. Time and again angry callers would demand to know how ACLU could defend a parade that would pass the homes of Jews and feature anti-Semitic speeches. By the same token, many of the callers praised Judge Wosik for preventing exactly that sort of activity.

Other errors of haste contributed, if less dramatically, to the fanciful debates. Collin was identified, early and often, as the leader of the "American Nazi Party," the organization from which he had been summarily ousted years before. ACLU was often portrayed as "supporting" Collin, a portrayal which is at best misleading.

All of the mistakes did nothing but enhance Collin's illusion. In the time it took to report on his plans, Collin became larger than life, a Neo-Nazi marshaling troops to assault a village. That odd perspective, coupled with the built-in fears that Collin's mere existence nurtures among Jews, created a broad debate having very little to do with reality.

By the end of the day — as David completed the appeal and sent it over to the Illinois appellate court — I was as frustrated and as angry as the callers with whom I was talking. The last of my conversations during that first day were frequently reduced to shouting matches, in which the callers hurled threats and I shouted facts or defenses.

At home that evening, I talked about the case and the calls with Sydney Weisman, the woman with whom my son and I lived (Sydney and I have since married). A Jew, Sydney had many of the same reservations I had been listening to all day. Her reservations, however, came in the form of questions rather than assertions; when her questions were answered, she agreed that ACLU had taken the right course and that my role within the controversy was the proper one. That support not only provided a sanctuary at home — one which David also enjoyed — it also suggested hope: if Sydney could listen and reason, so perhaps could others. My son, Jason, was not among the others; he concluded that a Nazi march offered nothing but danger and trouble for both Sydney and me and thus became the only person who disagreed with ACLU's position with whom I did not argue the point.

The television newscasts that evening treated the dispute as the headline story ("Nazi March on Skokie, Details at Ten") and added to the confusion by adopting symbols to portray the confrontation — swastika versus Star of David. The symbols, of course, were, like the reporting which followed, not entirely inaccurate; but they did not do much to put the confrontation in perspective.

On Friday the calls continued without letup. David's legal chores were, for the moment, completed, so he began to share the press inquiries with me. David did not take the nonpress calls, having adopted the position that, while ACLU should and would defend its position in public, that did not require spending the entire day on the phone with virulent critics. Since the calls were nasty enough and the issues were complex enough to merit attention, I did not want to push the calls off on anyone else on the staff, and for the balance of the controversy that pattern would prevail.

The press inquiries on Friday took two different courses. While the press still needed basic information and quotes, they also now believed that ACLU's defense of Fascists was part of the story as well. Thus, David and I spent the greatest portion of the day defending both Collin's right to demonstrate (a right which we continued to hold as absolute) and ACLU's reasons for providing a defense of that right. The barrage of calls had left us in a corner, so we argued our position from an increasingly hard-line posture, a posture which would do nothing to further anyone's understanding of the issues.

Late on Friday, the Illinois appellate court ruled. Without a single word of explanation, the court denied the appeal. Since the Illinois Supreme Court was not sitting at the time and since the appellate court had not ruled until the end of the business day, we concluded that there was nothing more to be done with the matter for the time being. Collin had established, beyond question, his intent to march in Skokie at some point in the future (thus insuring a continuing case within the courts), so we were sure that the litigation would not simply go away. Shellshocked, David and I went home for the weekend.

4

"No Free Speech for Fascists"

F rank Collin began the last weekend in April 1977 by announcing a new date for his proposed demonstration in Skokie. As soon as the appeals court refused to modify or vacate Judge Wosik's order, Collin told the press that he would demonstrate in Skokie on Saturday, April 30, instead of Sunday, May 1.

That announcement absolutely guaranteed that Collin would not be able to demonstrate in Skokie on the date he said he would. Whatever else the announcement was, it was perfectly self-defeating.

Collin's Friday afternoon announcement gave the people in Skokie ample time to reorganize against him. While the village's officials watched, somewhat amazed, news of Collin's new plan rippled through Skokie all night. By morning, the entire community was alerted and ready to meet Collin in front of the village hall at noon; in fact, some people had begun to gather in the neighborhood by nine o'clock. If anything, the urgency of the shortened notice added greater strength to those organizing against Collin; certainly the tension in Skokie on Saturday morning was at its highest pitch ever.

Skokie's Jewish community, which continued to be at the forefront of the organized opposition to Collin's demonstration, was by now not alone. They had been

71

joined by several left-wing anti-Fascist groups from Chicago, groups as anxious to confront Collin as Skokie's Jews were, although for entirely different reasons. The self-styled "radicals" came to Skokie on Saturday morning carrying two-by-four stakes into which they had driven ten-penny nails. To convince the local police that there was nothing untoward about the presence of those weapons, the anti-Facists had affixed small signs of protest to their bats.

The slogan under which the anti-Fascists gathered, which appeared at the top of the flyer in which they announced their opposition to Collin, was just as amusing as it was stupid. The headline on the flyer read "No Free Speech for Fascists."

"No free speech" is, of course, the hallmark of fascism. Advocating the revocation of free speech for Fascists is fascism itself, and roughly the same as advocating "no voting in a democracy." A surprising collection of leftists and others would eventually adopt the position represented by that slogan, most of them with a zeal sufficient to enable them to ignore the inherent contradiction of the position they had taken.

Between the contingent of people who seemed bent on a physical confrontation with Collin and his followers and the much larger contingent of people who would at least appear at the demonstration site, Skokie's officials were quickly convinced that Collin had to be stopped once again. The orderly demonstration which Collin claimed to seek was, in the judgment of Skokie's primary officials, not possible — a fact which may have saddened the officials more than it did Frank Collin. Skokie's officials might have assisted Frank Collin had he not taken his plan to the public. If they felt that they could get Collin in and out of the village with relative ease and quiet, they probably would have done so, for they believed that once Collin had his half-hour the issue would go away. One of Skokie's officials later told me that Collin could have gotten in and out of Skokie on Saturday morning had he not announced his intention to do so, but since he could not resist the temptation to get more press coverage, Collin gave the village's officials no choice.

Skokie's lawyers therefore went back into court on Saturday morning. They could not locate Judge Wosik in time — nor did they wish to waste time doing so — so they went instead to a Cook County judge who resides in Skokie. While Frank Collin was organizing his small band of followers for a motor caravan from Marquette Park to Skokie, Skokie's lawyers were arguing before Judge Harold Sullivan that Collin must, once again, be stopped.

Skokie's lawyers did not change their position in any way before Judge Sullivan. They continued to argue that the audience would become disorderly should Collin appear in the village, and from that fact they concluded that Collin should be stopped. Judge Sullivan, who heard no argument against Skokie's position because Collin was without representation at this "emergency" hearing, agreed. Sullivan expanded Wosik's order, banning Collin and NSPA from parading in uniform in Skokie "until further notice of the court."

As noon neared on Saturday, there were hundreds of people milling around the village hall, waiting for Collin. The village officials told the crowd that they had obtained an order which prevented Collin from coming into Skokie, but the crowd did not disperse. While they waited, Collin

73

and his followers drove to Skokie's border and onto an exit ramp, which was blocked by police cruisers.

Once the police had stopped Collin on the ramp, they served him with notice of Judge Sullivan's order. Collin informed his followers of the order, and then the entire contingent turned around and went back to NSPA's headquarters. Collin and his followers were accompanied back to their starting point by a substantial escort, including police (who made sure Collin obeyed the order of Judge Sullivan), reporters (who recorded everything on tape, paper, and film), and several cars from Skokie with citizen's band radios, which were used to relay back to the waiting crowd word of Collin's progress.

Skokie's officials, on the scene at the village hall, also reported Collin's trip to the crowd and the crowd, almost reluctantly, began to go home. By two o'clock, the neighborhood surrounding the village hall was back to a normal Saturday afternoon of shopping, traffic, and business as usual.

On Sunday, the date of Collin's originally scheduled demonstration, Collin and his band did not even bother to move. Collin had told the press that he would not violate any court order, a promise which made any attempt to demonstrate in Skokie futile.

The impact of Judge Sullivan's addition to Judge Wosik's order seemed, on the surface, minimal. It was not, however, for what Sullivan had done was to expand into permanency what had been a temporary order. Where Wosik had banned a specific demonstration, Sullivan had banned all demonstrations, creating an absolute ban on any assembly Collin might plan for Skokie. Such bans are so intolerable within the framework of the Bill of Rights that they rarely see the light of day. Judge Sullivan's order made the First Amendment, for all of its supposed power and strength, seem worthless.

The fact that Collin had not been represented in Sullivan's court made the order even more astonishing. Skokie's lawyers said that they had tried to inform David Goldberger of their intention to go back into court on Saturday morning but had been unable to locate him. David was, on that Saturday morning, exactly where he always is on Saturday mornings — working in his office at ACLU. Although it is doubtful that David's presence before Judge Sullivan would have made a difference in the outcome, since Sullivan's commitment to the First Amendment was obviously no greater than Wosik's, his absence was nevertheless greater evidence of the cavalier attitudes in the Illinois judiciary.

Although the events of the weekend left Frank Collin in a much more difficult position, they did nothing to weaken his illusory image. He had broken no law, yet Collin seemed to be lawless; he had done nothing more than read one piece of paper (and take action consistent with what he read), yet Collin seemed to be full of guile and cunning.

When he announced his Saturday demonstration, most people assumed that Collin was going to violate Judge Wosik's order. Even Judge Wosik himself eventually suggested that Collin *had* violated the order, although Wosik had enough sense to know that he could not make such a charge stick. Wosik's suggestion of contempt only reinforced his continuing image as a jurist with a limited command of the law, for by his own decree he had only banned Frank Collin from demonstrating on Sunday, May 1. No other date was mentioned by inference, nuance, or hint, and no other date was, therefore, covered. Even Frank Collin could read the four or five sentences it took to figure that out, and when he finished reading those sentences he came to the obvious conclusion — *all* other dates were available.

The public — relying on reports from the media which lacked any true depth — assumed that Wosik had simply banned Collin's demonstration. Thus, they generally assumed that Collin was breaking the law by going to Skokie on Saturday. Although that was simply not true, the image of Frank Collin as an outlaw was far stronger than the fairly obscure facts.

Similarly, the public ascribed to the selection of April 30 a sort of cunning which Collin does not normally exhibit. True guile would have driven Collin to keep his mouth shut so he could take the village by surprise *and* carry off his demonstration; true cunning would have dictated sneaky silence. However tauntingly cute Collin's new date seemed to be, the announcement of its selection bespeaks foolish planning and thoughtless talking rather than clever organizational strategy.

The most important aspect of Collin's sudden shift in the day of the demonstration, however, was in the impact it had on Skokie. The village thought itself at the mercy of the whims of a demented punk in spite of the court's protection, vulnerable on very short notice to any assault Collin chose to mount. The pressure that created on the village's officials was substantial enough to convince them that their court action — as completely successful as it had been — was not a sufficient defense against Frank Collin.

On Monday, May 2, the Skokie Village Council met to

draft — and pass — three ordinances. Each was aimed directly at Frank Collin, and each was based, in fact, on what the village council already knew about Collin's plan.

The first ordinance required a permit issued by the Village of Skokie for any parades on the streets or sidewalks of the village. To secure the required permit, all applicants would have to provide the village with thirty day's advance notice of the event and all applicants would also have to provide proof of possession of liability insurance against possible damage resulting from the proposed parade. The amount of insurance required was three hundred and fifty thousand dollars. The permit ordinance applied to any demonstration involving fifty or more individuals, a number, the village's officials would later testify, that could be composed of onlookers as well as demonstrators. The final provision of the ordinance was that the officials could waive any or all of the requirements at their own discretion.

The second ordinance made unlawful the public display of "symbols offensive to the community" and parades by political organizations in "military style" uniforms.

The third ordinance banned the distribution of literature containing "group libel." Group libel — a concept which only a lawyer could create and which only lawyers can admire — embraces the notion that it is possible to libel (defame, ridicule, derogate) a group sharing common traits such as ethnicity or religious beliefs. The concept deserves the lack of success it has met in courts, largely because it is usually used as an argument for censorship of such works as *Little Black Sambo* or

Huckleberry Finn. Skokie's council, of course, had in mind as the primary example of group libel nothing other than anti-Semitism.

Whatever else they turned out to be, the three new laws were certainly a perfect political response, for they reflected exactly the mood of the community. The laws even reflected — much too well, as it turned out — the panic that gripped Skokie when Collin changed his plans so suddenly. In their zeal to block Frank Collin, the village council passed laws of such sweeping range that everyone's rights were put in jeopardy. It is one of the saddest facts of the entire Skokie controversy that the village council did exactly what the most vocal segment of the community wanted it to do. By the time the council met, many citizens in Skokie were all too willing to give up their own rights rather than see Collin exercise his.

The ordinance requiring a demonstration permit was an absolute travesty. It allowed the village council to issue permits to anyone with whom that body agreed (through the waiver provision in the law), while enabling them to require an impossible insurance policy of anyone with whom they did not agree. The mechanism of censorship is perfect, for the insurance policy the ordinance required was virtually unobtainable; thus, the only people who could demonstrate in Skokie were those who could win the council's approval.

Since Frank Collin was hardly among those likely to win that approval, and since the council knew full well that he couldn't get the insurance, the problem facing the council was therefore solved. The problems facing the people of Skokie were hardly solved, however, for within months a group of Jewish war veterans discovered that they could not demonstrate *against* Frank Collin because of their failure to meet the requirements of the same ordinance which was drafted to stop Collin himself. The fact that the veterans elected not to sue the village in order to secure their rights only emphasizes the depth of the willingness among some in Skokie to trade their rights for some fleeting security.

The ban on "military style" uniforms is no less offensive to free expression, although it had the added virtue of being simply absurd. Not only was it unconstitutional because it constituted a prior restraint, the ban was so broad that it covered almost any demonstration — marching bands in political parades, Boy Scouts in the company of a senator, an American Legion contingent in a Fourth of July parade — including Collin's.

Finally, the group libel ordinance may have been satisfying to pass, but it did not even fit the circumstances which the council faced: Collin had not intended to distribute any more literature in Skokie, and the village could hardly prosecute him for distributing his flyer before the law had been passed. A large, cumbersome weapon at best, group libel in the form that the council adopted it did not even fit the circumstances.

The first reporter who called me for a reaction to the three ordinances had to read them to me. While he did I made some hasty notes, occasionally snorting at one or another provision. When he finished, he asked me for a general reaction to the package.

I paused for a moment before I answered, thinking about the events of the past few days as well as about the newest piece of the controversy. It was, from where I sat, a truly remarkable set of events: Wosik's seemingly tainted hearing and unconstitutional injunction, Sullivan's extension of prior restraint, the telephone calls (still coming into the office at a frantic pace), and now three broadly unconstitutional ordinances. The frustration and anger came out. I told the reporter that as far as I was concerned, "The Village of Skokie has shredded the First Amendment."

That sentence haunts me still. It came to be so widely quoted that it cemented, in spirit if not in reality, ACLU's public image for the remainder of the controversy. After long hours of discussion with David Goldberger, hours which took months to string together, I finally came to see my clever quote for what it was: arrogant nonsense. By then, of course, it was far too late.

The quote, which, I regret to note, so pleased me that I used it on dozens of occasions for days and days, reflected an attitude, a posture, which David and I brought to the confrontation. It was a posture which had always, in the past, suited us well, a posture which had also suited the issues well. It was built on the premise that those who preach changes in constitutional law are the enemy, possessed of sinister motive and intent. That rhetorical position, a product of the sixties without question, had always been effective; for that reason alone David and I fell into it quite naturally at the onset of the Skokie controversy.

The difficulty of that posture, we would discover a long time later, was that the Skokie controversy bore no resemblance whatsoever to the civil-rights confrontations of the sixties. There were no Bull Connors in Skokie, no sheriffs with cattle prods; there were certainly no deranged bureaucrats intent on sabotaging the nation through abuses of power in Skokie. Nevertheless David and I approached the issue from exactly that perspective.

Nothing reflected that mistake more vividly than my shredding quote. For months after I made that statement, people would attack me with it, arguing (quite properly) that it betrayed an absolute insensitivity to the specific issues of the controversy. While David and I did, eventually, develop the sensitivity that the issues demanded, our image remained firmly rooted in that initial stance we so easily adopted. The damage which that stance generated — in resignations, in hostility, in personal anguish — was as great as any generated by the actual controversy itself.

At the time, however, there was no room for such introspective flight. By the time the weekend's consequences had emerged, David and I were less than one day away from the special meeting of the Illinois board, scheduled two weeks before, at which the members would decide whether ACLU should represent Frank Collin or not.

As we prepared for that meeting, David and I approached for the first time the importance of the real issues in the controversy. We knew that Frank Collin could never find another lawyer at this late date, if only because we had seen enough of the adverse reaction to know that no lawyer in his right mind would *want* the case. We also knew that the stakes in the litigation were extremely high, for, if Skokie could prevail on any front, the law governing freedom of speech and assembly would be dramatically different.

Against that background, David and I quietly agreed that if the board voted to get out of the litigation, we would both resign. We could not continue to work for an

81

institution — our institution — if it would not hold to its time-honored position in this most difficult circumstance. Moreover, we were not prepared to let Frank Collin go unrepresented at any step in the pending litigation, a fact which would have made our continued employment with ACLU impossible if the board went against our position.

The gravity of that agreement shook us both. We both knew that ACLU was our home, our place to exist. The possibility that we might not belong there was terribly sad to contemplate.

Out of those sharp personal feelings and out of our firm belief in the correctness of our position on the issues, David and I lobbied our board of directors. We did so with dual intent. We wanted most of all to have an overwhelming majority of board members at the meeting, for anything less than complete support would leave ACLU in a terribly weak and probably untenable position; we also wanted our now public position fully supported, so that while we urged all to attend, we also urged our position upon them.

The board met on Thursday, May 4, just far enough away from the hectic weekend to have all the various pieces in place yet close enough to the events to see the results — the flashing telephone lights and the haggard office faces — of those events. There was a solid majority of the board in attendance, and the debate was quiet, deliberate, and earnest.

Edwin Rothschild began the meeting with an extensive recitation of the facts in the controversy. He had not been in the office during the activity, but he had been in constant touch with either David or me from the outset. As a result, Edwin worked through the case with none of the emotion that David or I would have used. In spite of his objectivity, however, Rothschild made little effort to conceal his position in the matter. He made sure that the board understood from the outset that a vote to bail out would be a vote in opposition to Rothschild's own command to the staff. In a coldly political sense, the chairman told his board that they would have to go through the staff and the chair to change the public policy.

None of that — not our lobbying, not Rothschild's hard line — was needed. The board (as David later described it) held their noses and voted to continue ACLU's efforts in the case.

The vote was unanimous. There had been no serious consideration given to any position other than the one that the organization had already taken. Since ACLU had, with rare and admittedly erroneous exceptions, always stood firmly for the proposition that basic rights belong to all, the Illinois board had little choice in the matter, but their vote was as much an affirmation of that principle as it was the product of it. David and I left the meeting with the grim satisfaction of knowing that we would, at least, sink with the organization we cherished instead of having to sink without it.

The Illinois board voted to support a simple proposition, in the end, at the same time they voted to support an incredibly complex set of issues. In voting to continue the litigation against Skokie's various attempts to censor Collin, the Illinois board had really done nothing more than read, and support, the First Amendment. Where the ACLU board read that government "shall make no law" abridging free expression, it had assumed that "no law" means just that and voted accordingly.

That vote, however, plunged the organization into a remarkable labyrinth of legal paths full of twists and turns, for in less than one week the Skokie litigation had exploded, bursting into several large pieces.

The ordinances, passed by the village on May 2, created an entirely new shape for the landscape of the Skokie litigation. In passing the ordinances, the village council had absolutely destroyed the need for Judge Wosik's modified injunction. Skokie's lawyers had argued to Wosik (and again to Judge Sullivan) that they needed the protection of the injunction because violence seemed inevitable if the proposed demonstration took place. Although they never quite said so, the village's lawyers also implied that they were somehow powerless to prevent that imminent lawlessness. The three ordinances, of course, blew those special arguments right out of the water.

The ordinances gave Skokie the absolute power to control the time, place, and location of all demonstrations in the village. With that power, and with the ample notice of any demonstration required by the permit ordinance, Skokie's officials clearly held control over Collin's proposed demonstration. Either they could hold Collin off, conceivably forever, with the permit/insurance scheme, or, barring that, the village could arrest Collin if and when he failed to obey either of the other two ordinances. Since the village had passed both of those ordinances after a careful review of Frank Collin's announced plan for his demonstration, they *knew* he would violate them; thus protected, the village retained little if any need for the continued protection of the court.

The injunction itself, unconstitutional in its original form, now of course covered all future demonstrations by Collin in Skokie. What had been a narrow ban on a single event had exploded into a virtual permanent ban on any events under any circumstances—absolute censorship had been fashioned from Judge Wosik's ban. However offensive to free speech Judge Wosik's order had been, the modification made it utterly intolerable.

David Goldberger, working bearishly enough to have by now roared at least once at every person in the office, skillfully meshed the old, simple First Amendment arguments with the new issues arising from the ordinances and the modification of Wosik's order. The entire package was prepared in anticipation of an Illinois Supreme Court review of the matter.

The injunction was nearly two weeks old by the time the Illinois Supreme Court said anything about the matter. When that court spoke, it merely whispered its contempt for justice and then faded from sight.

The Illinois Supreme Court discovered, its motives subject only to guess, a procedural quirk in the state's judicial system that enabled the highest court in the state to duck the issue altogether. They used that quirk to do precisely that, ruling on no question other than a procedural one. The procedural question arose from odd circumstances, but it turned out to be among the most critical of the early judicial problems in the controversy.

The question, simply stated, was "May Frank Collin have permission to by-pass the state appellate court in order to be heard by the Illinois Supreme Court?" The Illinois Supreme Court said No.

Because the appellate court had not yet ruled on the

injunction itself but had only refused to hear speedy arguments about it, thus leaving the order in force by inaction, it still held technical jurisdiction over the case. The severe nature of the litigation, however, demanded hasty review at the highest judicial levels of the state. For that reason, David sought a hearing with the supreme court, a hearing which would, when completed, resolve the legal issues of the case permanently insofar as Illinois was concerned. The supreme court declined to listen, however, telling Collin instead to wait his turn for an appellate hearing.

Such contempt for a matter involving the most precious of American rights was stunning. The Illinois Supreme Court had said, in effect, "Never mind that the First Amendment is being violated every day the injunction is in force, several more weeks won't matter." There is but one resort available to Americans treated in this way by state courts, and early in June David Goldberger filed on behalf of Frank Collin a petition seeking emergency assistance from United States Supreme Court Justice John Paul Stevens.

Mr. Justice Stevens was, perhaps, driven to drastic action by the drastic inaction of Illinois. Whatever his reasons, Stevens took an emergency petition, which he alone was empowered to act upon and which only he had been asked to consider, and expanded it to a petition for *certoriari* (a petition for a ruling on the merits of the issue). He then presented the matter to the entire United States Supreme Court. It is most probable that Stevens, at that time brand new to the Court and by far the most junior of the justices, did not want to exercise anything other than caution, for which reason he sought the assistance of the full Court. The Supreme Court's reaction was remarkable.

On June 14, the United States Supreme Court ruled that any citizen subject to prior restraint of speech is entitled to have that restraint either reviewed or removed immediately. If the injunction against a citizen remains in force, the Court held, the state has an absolute obligation to provide a rapid review of the injunction. The law having been thus interpreted, the Court ordered Illinois — through the Illinois Supreme Court — to provide an expeditious hearing on Skokie's still-standing injunction.

As soon as it became public, the Supreme Court ruling was the lead story for every news outlet in greater Chicago. The follow-up stories and in-depth analyses held the story in prominence for the remainder of that day and for at least two days thereafter. What had been a slow and boring story about a case wandering through the Illinois judiciary had suddenly become a ruling from the entire Supreme Court. Once the press began to work the story, the public perceptions of the controversy shifted once again.

Skokie was stunned by the ruling. In their zeal to halt Collin, most of Skokie's Jewish population had all but convinced themselves that he had absolutely no rights at all. Now, no matter how they *felt,* that conviction was no longer legally valid. Moreover, to the shock of Skokie and most of Chicago as well, the Court had made no bones about the fact that Frank Collin — Nazi or not — has the same rights as any other citizen. That harsh reality meant, many began to suspect, that perhaps Collin was entitled to demonstrate in Skokie. The ruling was only a first, tentative signal, but it surely seemed to be a signal nevertheless.

ACLU's telephone came alive once more. There had been a week or so of relative quiet after the first roaring rush of calls, which had lasted about two weeks. That quiet now disappeared under a flood of press inquiries and protest calls.

The content of the newest round of protests had changed somewhat. While the anger was always present and while the vast majority of callers continued to identify themselves as Jews, the principal objection to ACLU was now speed rather than position. The anger that grew from the Supreme Court's ruling was directed at ACLU, because we had taken the case there with what many believed to be unseemly haste.

Because we had not yet recognized the dangers of our fierce defense of First Amendment rights, because we still thought of (and I certainly spoke of) Skokie as the "enemy," the Court's ruling seemed to somehow affirm both our aggression and our lack of respect for the villagers. It was in this round of calls, in fact, that I found my "shredding" quote coming back at me time and again, and the Jewish community without question saw a direct relation between my quote and the Court's ruling. In the parlance of public relations experts, our image was shot.

Lacking any time in which to really figure out what was going on and lacking any other effective response, David and I took to expressing quiet gallows humor. As the public called to accuse us of everything from genocide to sodomy, I kept reminding David that "as long as they spell our names right" we were getting good press. David more often than not responded by asking, a grim chuckle in his tone, what I thought the office would be like with but two people in it.

We also joked, as much from fear as from relief, about the most vicious of the protest calls — those which dealt with our respective religious beliefs. I recounted for David the truly grim nature of those calls, but I also pointed out the deliciously circular logic which they contained.

That logic held that David Goldberger could not participate in the controversy because he is a Jew and thus morally precluded from protecting the First Amendment rights of a Nazi; at the same time, the logic held that I was also precluded from participation in the defense of those rights because I am not Jewish and, therefore, far too insensitive to the issues of nazism. I pointed out to those who followed that logic that their reasoning meant that *nobody* could represent Collin, since everybody is either Jewish or not. At least two of the callers on whom I used that reply simply hung up.

However illogical, the protest calls nevertheless continued to come in. In the wake of the Supreme Court's ruling, there was another week of steady calls, followed by months in which the calls came at a rate of only a dozen or so per week. The calls were not the only form the protests took. David found that he could not lunch outside the office without having to explain — if not defend — ACLU's position on the "Skokie" controversy, and we both discovered that the highly visible nature of the entire debate made us fair game in all places at all times. People who had recognized me (from television, I assumed) and wanted to say something about "Skokie" started conversations on commuter trains as I rode home from work.

In this same period, I also received a ticket from the police in my community, issued for my admitted failure to purchase a local tax sticker for my car. I made the required purchase, but I could not avoid the court date, so I took a morning off from work to go face the court and prove that I had corrected my sin. The traffic court judge asked me the usual questions in such matters, and I, in turn, showed him my receipts for the stickers. He dismissed the case, but as I left he stopped me.

"Mr. Hamlin," said the Judge, "are you with the ACLU?"

I froze, entirely unsure of what I ought to reply and tensely angry at having been once again confronted with my work in entirely inappropriate circumstances. It crossed my mind to say, "It's none of your damn business," but instead I turned to face the judge and said, "I am, your Honor."

"Well, young man," he said, "we disagree with what you do, but we recognize your right to do it."

"I feel exactly the same way about you, your Honor," I snapped testily. The judge laughed, thankfully ignoring my intended slur, and I turned to leave once again. I looked at the faces in the court and saw, to my instant horror, a reporter from the Chicago *Tribune* in the front row. The reporter, with a restraint I still appreciate, did not use the encounter as the basis for yet another story about the fallout of "Skokie."

At the time, it was the only restraint the press seemed willing to exercise. With the intervention of the United States Supreme Court, the press had shed all doubt and created of the controversy a full-blown, grand-scale, no-coverage-is-too-much media event. The controversy already had all the elements of a perfect media event: stark symbols and combatants; high drama, emotion, and building tension; and, with the intervention of the Supreme Court in such dramatic fashion, national importance.

All of the old errors continued without change. The demonstration in Skokie always became a "March" in headlines; the reporters covering the story continued to report about a "parade" in Skokie or a "march through" the village. A reporter with the Chicago *Sun-Times* who was assigned to the story during this period called me several times about it — six months later that same reporter called me to ask if the report he had gotten from a *Cleveland* newspaper was accurate. The report he was trying to confirm was a precisely accurate description of Collin's demonstration; thus, a reporter for a major Chicago daily newspaper was writing about Skokie during this period without having the slightest idea of what Collin's plan held.

The attention given the controversy grew to encompass every imaginable aspect of the story. Holocaust survivors living in Skokie were interviewed over and over again about their experiences during the Second World War; the barrage of criticism at ACLU had become part of the story as well, and the press now constantly asked how many calls we were getting, what the "protests" were like, and so forth. National columnists began to write about the issues, editorials started to appear across the country, letters to editors filled Chicago's papers every day — the public was without question well (if not wisely) informed.

There was, finally, no place to hide from the controversy. With the constant attention of the media, the issue had become so closely tied to ACLU that every employee from our office encountered people who commented — often harshly, sometimes nastily — on "Skokie." The intensity of the controversy led to almost daily "Skokie stories" in the office: someone had ruined an otherwise pleasant dinner party by asking a staff member about the controversy and generating a huge argument; a friendship had been badly strained with a heated discussion of the issues; a relative had called to ask what the hell was going on — nobody could escape.

Elsewhere in the country, ACLU's participation in the case had also drawn enormous attention. The Jewish Defense League in New York responded by staging a sit-in at the National Headquarters of the ACLU; another Jewish organization occupied the Florida ACLU office (prompting the director there to call me, angrily demanding an explanation); the JDL also moved into the Los Angeles office for a time. Our office in Chicago was occupied, for about an hour, late one Friday afternoon by a group of about a dozen anti-Fascists, who (among other things) could not seem to keep straight whether they were mad at us over Skokie or abortion.

While the attention was uncomfortable for ACLU and those of us in the office in Chicago, it must have been a source of glee for Frank Collin, for we were but peripheral players, whereas Frank Collin stood at center stage. Collin's pure outrageousness together with Skokie's granite resolve to stop his demonstration created a huge new illusion: Collin had become the nation's most prominent villain.

It was hardly the calculated manipulation of an entire press corps which put Collin in the spotlight; rather, Collin simply *existed*, which was more than enough for the press, particularly since Skokie's population was treating Collin's existence as a serious threat. All he had to do was continue to exist, and Frank Collin could enjoy the attention of a nation. For that reason alone, I am convinced, Frank Collin reinforced the illusion by announcing as his next proposed demonstration date in Skokie the Fourth of July, 1977.

What followed that announcement was shameless manipulation by the Illinois courts. In order to make absolutely sure that Frank Collin's constitutionally protected demonstration could not take place as planned, the Illinois judiciary engaged in near contempt of the United States Supreme Court.

The Supreme Court ruling of June 14 commanded either that the injunction against Collin be expeditiously reviewed or lifted. The Illinois Supreme Court, upon learning of that ruling, passed the word down to the appellate court, which set a hearing date. That exceedingly complex set of actions took the Illinois judiciary more than two weeks to accomplish, two weeks which enabled the appellate court to set a hearing for the *Sixth of July, 1977.*

I can imagine no more shocking behavior. In reply to an order from the U.S. Supreme Court, a state judiciary willfully ignores the spirit (and, by their failure to lift the injunction, the letter) of the law of the land. In the process, the Illinois judiciary also managed to trample once again the very right the Court sought to protect with its procedural command. I told every reporter who called that there was no evident relationship between the principles of justice and the judges in Illinois.

That harsh criticism drew a single, misinformed response. One of the three judges who eventually heard the appeal took time to chide David Goldberger for the comments I had made, attributing them to the wrong David. Beyond that, there was silence. The Illinois bar

93

had evidently learned, from David Goldberger and from ACLU, that the price of defending the rights of Nazis is public vilification, whereas the price of silence is serenity.

By the time it finally took place, the appeal hearing seemed a miraculous achievement. The hearing did take place, however, and just as David Goldberger had adjusted and refined his arguments, so had Skokie. Before the appellate court, Skokie's lawyers raised a new, artfully drawn argument, an argument which rested on the world's most hated symbol.

Gilbert Gordon argued the appeal for the Village of Skokie. He began by covering the old arguments, which had served the village quite well before Judges Wosik and Sullivan. If Frank Collin were to demonstrate in Skokie, Gordon argued, there might well be a violent audience reaction; and if the speaker is in danger of being attacked by the audience, he should be prevented from speaking.

To the heckler's veto argument, however, Gordon added new material. He suggested to the court that the display of the swastika in the village of Skokie would constitute "fighting words." If the court would not ban Collin altogether, Gordon argued, then the court must at least ban his symbol.

Gordon was most effective. He made abundantly clear the village's wish to have the entire injunction upheld, but he provided the court with an option by suggesting that they could surely get away with a ban on the swastika in any event.

The introduction of the "fighting words" doctrine into the litigation required some unique contortions. The theory, for one thing, had never before been applied to anything other than actual words; Skokie had somehow expanded the standing definition to include symbols. Moreover, the "fighting words" doctrine had heretofore been applied exclusively to one-on-one confrontations (typically, when a demonstrator called a policeman something which evoked a physical response instantly). Skokie sought for the first time in history to grossly expand the doctrine to demonstrations and audiences.

The most difficult twist of the doctrine, however, lay with Skokie's use of it as a vehicle for prior restraint. By its very nature, the doctrine of "fighting words" comes into play only *after* the words themselves have been uttered; Skokie sought to use a post-speech defense doctrine as an offensive weapon of prior restraint.

In reply to those new twists of the doctrine, David Goldberger noted that Skokie's reading of the concept was at considerable variance with the concept itself, but he relied most heavily on the single strand of legal logic that, he told the court, held all of Skokie's arguments together.

That single strand was the audience reaction: whether to the symbols or to the demonstrators, both of Skokie's arguments required the audience to react. So long as that remained true, David argued, Skokie would be in the absolutely impossible position of attempting to predict the future while at the same time ignoring the command of the First Amendment.

If all that is required to prevent a speech is the threat of a violent reaction, David argued, then no idea will be safe ever again. On any side of any argument, there may be those willing to threaten disruption of the other's activity, a threat which by Skokie's logic would be sufficient to halt the activity before it could take place. The

First Amendment commands precisely the opposite course: let the speech take place and then arrest anyone who breaks the law.

David concluded his arguments to the appellate court with a quiet suggestion that, for freedom of speech to have any meaning or value, it must apply equally to both popular and unpopular ideas. If free speech is truly free, Goldberger said to the court, it must be free here and now to protect this most vile of citizens or it will inevitably be available to none.

Although there was no legal precedent at all for the use of "fighting words" as a doctrine of prior restraint, the appellate court nevertheless adopted Skokie's theory, lifting the injunction's ban on uniforms while substituting a ban on the display of the swastika in Skokie.

There was, however, ample legal precedent, flowing directly from the First Amendment itself, for an end to the injunction. There was also the clear, direct mandate of the U.S. Supreme Court to act rapidly on the restraint under any circumstances. Nevertheless, the appellate court ignored the First Amendment and, once again, distorted the Supreme Court's order. The appellate court not only left the injunction in force, it also ruled that Skokie could have made an argument holding that Collin's demonstration presented a "clear and present danger." Since Skokie had neglected to raise that argument, the appellate court ruled, the entire case would go back to Judge Wosik for further hearings on that very issue. Directed by the U.S. Supreme Court to adjudicate the prior restraint expeditiously, the three-judge panel sent the case back to the lower court for more hearings, not on the merits of the injunction but on a new argument in support of that injunction, which was the least expeditious route imaginable or available.

David Goldberger responded to the ruling by announcing an appeal to be filed with the Illinois Supreme Court. Skokie's officials said they welcomed the appeal, content for the moment to let the entire debate reach a "deliberate" conclusion within the courts. Frank Collin announced that he would not violate the newest modifications of the injunction, insisting instead on his right to display his symbols, a right for which he was prepared to wait.

Since the Illinois Supreme Court was not in session at the time, the injunction would remain in force until at least the middle of September. There, with the willing assistance of the Illinois judiciary, the matter of the injunction against Frank Collin rested. It would be 1978 before the Illinois Supreme Court finally ruled on the matter.

There can be no more telling evidence of the power of Frank Collin's illusion than the performance of the Illinois judiciary in the litigation surrounding Skokie's injunction. From Judge Wosik through the entire chain of jurists who touched the case, there was a willingness to ignore the law and abuse the most vital rights in this nation. The judges who handled the case, in concert, prevented a perfectly legal, absolutely constitutional political expression.

5

"Agony after Agony"

The impact of Frank Collin's illusion upon the Jewish community of Chicago was far, far greater than any which that illusion worked upon the Illinois judiciary. Although Collin was able to misdirect the jurists of the state well enough to cause serious lapses in judgment, he drew from the Jews of Chicago a response that made injustice pale in comparison: Collin caused the Jewish community to panic.

By the end of the summer of 1977, the evidence of that panic was everywhere to be seen. Confronted directly with a shadowy reminder of Hitler, the Jewish community so overreacted that black became white, principle became expedience, fiction became fact.

There are ample, valid explanations for the panic. The years of ceaseless threats to the security of Israel had, by 1977, begun to take their toll on the politics of America, and surely the blurry threat Collin seemed to present to the Jews in Skokie was hard to distinguish from the threat which confronted the Jewish community's other homeland. Collin, as well, opened as widely as possible the door to anti-Semitism, bringing that particular brand of hatred into the light for a moment.

The reaction to the anti-Semitism Collin personifies was based, without question, on years of much less open hatred. Like racism or sexism, anti-Semitism never seems to go away in America; rather it festers just beneath the political waters, always present and always foul. Most anti-Semitism is far more subtle than Collin's; in reacting to him the Jewish community surely vented other, older angers, too — for all anti-Semitism in all forms, the Jewish community rose up to confront Frank Collin.

With the help of the media, Collin had all but become the Hitler clone he half wanted to be. Because he wanted them to, the Jewish community reacted to Collin as if he were responsible for the holocaust. Because there is, with ample historical justification, a part of every Jew which supports the JDL's battle cry, "Never Again," the reaction to Collin became far greater than the threat Collin actually presented.

The grim history which Frank Collin personifies surely led to the firmness with which the Jewish community resolved to prevent his demonstration, but at the same time Collin generated a wave of fearful anger, anger that was directed not only at Frank Collin but at anyone who stood near him at any time. By that definition, ACLU and ACLU's employees were easy targets; as the early rush of hateful calls had signaled, those of us willing to defend Collin's rights were going to be subjected to the hatred which Collin generates.

That anger surfaced quickly, and the telephone calls were but a quiet warning. Shortly after Judge Wosik's very first ruling in the controversy, groups began calling ACLU to request speakers who would "talk about Skokie." The first batch of those requests was typical of all the requests which followed. There were speaker requests from several high schools, a law school, a senior citizen organization, and a dozen or more Jewish groups. Sheila Meyer, ACLU's administrator in charge of the speaker's bureau (among other things), took every request to David or me, and we split them up. Later, a few board members also accepted engagements on the issue.

Among the first of the engagements I accepted was one in a high school which educates a sizable portion of the children of Skokie. The assembled students were clearly troubled by the issue, and one of their teachers told me that the pressure the students were under from their parents and grandparents was substantial. It was understandable, then, that their questions were at once tentative and faintly angry. Among the assembled teachers, however, there was open contempt for ACLU's position, contempt which caused some of the adults in the room to attack me as stupid, dishonest, and cruel.

A few days later, sharing the podium with Skokie lawyer Harvey Schwartz, I stood before a group of students in the University of Chicago's vaunted school of law. There, one of the students did not like the answer I gave to his question, so he responded by telling me to get the fillings in my teeth changed from gold to silver so I could "go to the end of the line when Collin opens the camps."

On an evening late in June, I stood before several hundred noisy, restless, visibly angry Jews assembled in a synagogue in Skokie. I had been threatened over this particular engagement ("If you come to Skokie, you son of a bitch, you won't go home," the caller had said), and when I reported the threat to Skokie's police, they took it quite seriously. I fully expected somebody in that audience to attack me. I was thoroughly, absolutely terrified.

101

The audience was assembled to hear a panel discussion of the controversy. Among the panel were Erma Gans, the holocaust survivor who spoke for "Concerned Jewish Citizens"; Gilbert Gordon, the village's other attorney; Paul Franklin, who represented the Anti-Defamation League of B'nai B'rith; and someone called a "moderator," a word I presumed to be most optimistically chosen. The format, which called for brief opening remarks from each panel member and written questions from the audience thereafter, put me at the podium first.

Before I spoke a word, an angry man in the middle of the auditorium rose out of his seat and began to shout and move toward the stage. He was restrained by ushers and some of the people around him, while I fell back from the podium to wait out the disruption. While I waited a man in the very first row caught my eye and smiled as he gave me the finger; in the back of the room somebody shouted at me to "stop being so arrogant," a taunt which drove me back to the podium.

Again the room exploded as I began to speak and again I moved back. This time I was content to wait much longer, calculating that a longer wait away from the podium reduced the amount of time I spent at the podium. When I finally got to speak, I rushed through one or two points (leaving for some other time the five or six others I had intended to make) and then moved as quickly as I could to the panelists' table, where I thought there might be some security in numbers.

The mood of the audience remained tensely angry for the duration of the evening. When Erma Gans let loose her militant mixture of anti-nazism and fanciful images of Frank Collin, the audience responded lustily, encouragement rippling through the room. When Gilbert Gordon reaffirmed the village's willingness to prevent Collin's demonstration through court action, he was cheered; when he then said that the village would, if necessary, arrest anybody who broke the law, including Collin's audience, they turned on him, jeering and booing loudly.

A few people in the audience agreed with ACLU's position. Sheila Meyer, from our office, was there and so were Frank Haiman (my most cherished teacher and friend from ACLU's board) and Sydney, my housemate and staunchest supporter. All three of them told me that I did a credible job that night. I remember only blurred images and a vivid fear, but not a word of what I said.

The evening's discussion ended, and, as quickly as it did, I was escorted by some of the synagogue's leaders and a Skokie policeman to a side exit that led to the basement of the building. There, in the company of my escort and Paul Franklin (the ADL's representative on the panel), I waited while the crowd dispersed and another of the synagogue's leaders located Sydney and led her down to join us. When the police were satisfied that we could leave, Sydney and I walked to our car in the middle of a moving corridor of plainclothesmen. A cruiser followed us to the village's boundary, after which we took a most circuitous route home.

It was not always so dramatic, but the anger of the Jewish community was never far from sight. David Goldberger's parents heard their son denounced by the rabbi in their own synagogue; Frank Haiman watched, amazed, as a rabbi demonstrated a point by swinging his fist at Haiman, stopping just short of Frank's nose; board members began to complain of being openly baited and insulted

103

in social gatherings. A caller from Boston told me that, if Collin marched on Skokie, he and his friends "from the Jewish ghetto" were coming to find me; David on one or two occasions felt the need of a bodyguard while giving a speech, and on one occasion the tumult in the audience prompted the guard to leap up to protect his charge bodily.

In our own office, the anger arrived every day with the morning mail. A correspondent wrote to me that it was "too bad your parents, brother or sister, wife and children weren't exterminated by the Nazis." A man named Shuriff wrote from New York to award me the "Bastard Award of the Century," going on to tell me that "my only wish for you is that you suffer through the remainder of your life as you experience agony after agony." David Goldberger's mail was, if anything, nastier and slightly more voluminous than mine.

The emotional assault which grew out of the controversy was but one aspect of the response of the Jewish community. Frank Collin drew from his target audience an intellectual response as well, one which took two separate courses. While Jews across the country began to resign their memberships in ACLU, the Jewish community in Chicago decided to file another suit against Frank Collin.

The litigation was filed in Cook County Chancery Court in the latter part of the summer of 1977. It was the product of the work of several Chicago-area Jewish organizations, chief among them the Anti-Defamation League. The suit was filed on behalf of the class of citizens in Skokie known as "survivors of the holocaust," and it claimed that a demonstration by Frank Collin in Skokie would constitute a tort known as "menticide" and that he should, therefore, be barred from demonstrating. The class

104

of survivors was represented in the actual litigation by Sol Goldstein, the man who had testified before Judge Wosik for Skokie.

A tort is a civil (not criminal) wrong. "Menticide" was made up by the lawyers working on the suit, who, with the help of some psychiatrists supporting their work, defined it as "the willful infliction of emotional harm." Menticide occurs, according to the litigation's theory, during the process of resurrecting the emotional and psychological responses to the original holocaust.

Goldstein v. *Collin* was in every imaginable way a remarkable lawsuit. It was filed precisely when it was needed least. It had as its chief sponsor and proponent an organization which had, for years, advocated the same First Amendment position which ACLU held: no censorship. The principal witness in the litigation, Sol Goldstein, put his name to a theory his very own actions betrayed. Although the very heart of the case was a most sensitive and delicate point — survivors do, in fact, carry deep emotional and psychological scars — the lawyer sent into the courts to advocate that delicate point was an insensitive fanatic. That lawyer took into the courts litigation which was founded on several false premises. In all, the litigation seemed to be an even more drastic reaction to Frank Collin than the most vile attacks on ACLU.

The so-called "survivor suit" was filed in the latter part of the summer. At the time the litigation was presented to the chancery court, Judge Wosik's injunction was in full force and, with the Sullivan modification, preventing Frank Collin's demonstration for the untold future. All three of the Skokie ordinances were also in full force, and, since no challenge had yet been filed against

105

them in any court, the village was free to arrest Collin for violating them the moment he appeared in Skokie. There was, in short, absolutely no way for Frank Collin to appear in Skokie; he would violate the court's orders if he tried and break Skokie's laws if he actually got to the village. With all of that existing protection, Jewish groups nevertheless went to court to prevent Frank Collin from demonstrating in Skokie.

The litigation, moreover, asked for injunctive relief from the proposed demonstration, seeking in effect a carbon copy of Wosik's order. Since the order they sought was already in place when they sought it, the litigation was absolutely redundant before it was even filed.

Goldstein v. *Collin* was redundant in yet another respect. Since Sol Goldstein was a resident of Skokie, he was being represented in the courts at the time he filed his suit on the very matter his suit dealt with. The only logical reason for filing a suit which duplicated Skokie's official efforts would be a lack of confidence in their work; if Goldstein felt that Skokie's lawyers were not doing an adequate job, then he would logically file his own suit. Yet as he filed the suit, Skokie's lawyers were doing *exactly* what Sol Goldstein asked the court to do, and they had not yet failed in any attempts to halt the demonstration.

However confusing the intent of the litigation, its sponsorship was abundantly clear. Along with some other Jewish groups in Chicago, the Anti-Defamation League of B'nai B'rith was a principal moving force behind the suit. The executive director of the Midwest ADL office, Abbott Rosen, spent the several months after the filing of the litigation defending it before audience after

106

audience. His defense of the litigation was every bit as vigorous as his opposition to it had been just weeks before.

Paul Franklin, the ADL staff lawyer who had shared the table with me in the Skokie synagogue, had joined me in the basement of that building to wait out the crowds because he had fared no better with the audience than had I. Paul Franklin had, in fact, advocated exactly the same position as I had that evening (getting the same boos and jeers), and he had done so as a representative of the ADL. He was, in those early weeks of the public debate over Skokie, but one of several ADL representatives to be treated like an enemy by the very constituency he purported to represent.

The time-honored and well-tested position of the Anti-Defamation League had, until Skokie, always been essentially the same as that of ACLU, although the ADL added to its position on the First Amendment a purely self-protective clause. In addition to the long-standing belief that the greatest threat to Jews anywhere is the loss of freedom, the ADL also firmly endorsed the notion that overreacting to Neo-Nazis only gives them more attention than they deserve in the first place. At the same time, since shunning neo-nazism is not protection enough by itself, the ADL around the country has always been the best available monitor of Neo-Nazi activity. While they stood vigilant against groups like Collin's, the ADL also held firm to a belief in complete political freedom.

That same organization, advocating the same position, had been raked over the coals in public gatherings for weeks by the time Paul Franklin arrived in the synagogue basement with me. Franklin and Abbott Rosen had spent

hours with Jewish groups, trying to persuade them to
measure their response to Collin carefully while at the
same time giving their accurate, belittling analysis of
Collin and NSPA. As Franklin had discovered that evening
in Skokie, however, others, including Erma Gans, were
offering a very different vision of Frank Collin, a vision
which was certainly out of touch with reality but very
much in touch with the fears and emotions of the Jewish
community.

In the zealous atmosphere that pervaded Skokie it was
indeed true that anyone who advocated freedom for Frank
Collin was the enemy; in the first month or so of the
controversy, the enemy was composed of ACLU and ADL.
Quickly enough, however, ACLU stood alone.

The organization which had for years advocated a pure
First Amendment position and which had sought to
minimize the attention given to Neo-Nazi groups came
to Cook County Chancery Court advocating prior restraint
of speech and offering more publicity for nazism than
even Frank Collin could hope for.

The promise of excessive publicity for nazism came
from the chief counsel in the survivor litigation, a bombastic, aggressive, artless lawyer named Jerome Torshen.
As quickly as he found himself in front of a judge, Torshen
promised to bring before the court a parade of witnesses
who would relive in vivid detail every tormenting aspect
of the holocaust, a parade which Torshen said would convince the court that Collin must not be allowed to appear
in Skokie. With that promise, the Anti-Defamation League
had turned completely against the same position they had
advocated not three weeks earlier.

The litigation itself is evidence of the air of panic which

must have attended its preparation, for it is overflowing with flaws, distortions, and improbabilities. As a class action, the litigation by its very existence argued several principles which were simply not true.

By claiming to represent the entire class of holocaust survivors, the ADL implied that all survivors would be harmed by the demonstration. The harm would be triggered by the presence of uniforms and symbols almost exactly like those worn by the Nazis, who had caused the original harm. On that entirely implausible foundation rested a substantial portion of the theory in the case.

For one thing, the class action ignored the possibility that one or more survivors in Skokie might not see the demonstration. That obvious fact presented multiple problems for the litigation. It suggested, first, that there might not actually be a "class" which could be said to be facing imminent harm, but rather that only some unspecified members of the class might be harmed. If that were the case, would it not be more prudent (and far more constitutional) for the court to invite those harmed by the demonstration to sue after the harm had taken place?

The only sure way for all survivors to be victims of menticide would be for all survivors to attend Frank Collin's demonstration. There is nothing — not the Bill of Rights, not any civil or criminal law, not even residence in Skokie — which requires anyone to see a public demonstration which they do not wish to see. Thus, the survivor litigation implied — without actually saying so — that presence at the demonstration was not required for the harm to take place. By insisting that the class would be harmed as a total group while ignoring the possibility that some of the class might not even be anywhere near

Collin at any time, the suit forced the conclusion that a survivor could be harmed without attending the demonstration.

If that indirect harm takes place, the potential causes of it are hardly confined to Frank Collin. If all that is required for menticide to take place is the presentation, direct or indirect, of symbols and uniforms or other reminders of nazism, then the Goldstein litigation swept more broadly than even Skokie's most militant officials were prepared to sweep. At an absolute minimum, the theory of menticide led directly to the censorship of **film** of Nazi demonstrations broadcast over television channels reaching Skokie; it led as well to censorship of photographs of Nazis in uniform available to survivors in the village. By the suit's very own definition, in fact, the evidence Jerome Torshen threatened to put on the witness stand was every bit as menticidal as Frank Collin's demonstration.

The proponents of the use of menticide as a device for censoring speech insisted that their theory was actually very limited in scope, narrow enough to protect Skokie but hardly broad enough to be used as a general tool of suppression. Abbott Rosen and Jerome Torshen and others insisted that the censorship they advocated was designed to help the "unique concentration of survivors" in Skokie exclusively, that without such a concentration the theory would not work. That is the traditional position of anyone who advocates abridgments of basic rights — "it's O.K., folks, we're tampering with the other guy's rights, but we aren't going to tamper with yours." It was no more valid in the hands of Torshen or Rosen than it was in the hands of Richard Nixon.

In fact, the claim for a uniquely narrow reading of menticide exploded within months of the filing of the suit, for soon enough the theory had been used to censor a television news broadcast in Philadelphia, Pennsylvania. Although Philadelphia is some considerable distance from Skokie and probably has a much less concentrated survivor community, the same theory Torshen and Rosen said was special to Skokie took "Black Perspectives on the News" off the air. The incident occurred when Frank Collin taped a segment of that program, and holocaust survivors in Philadelphia promptly sued to have the show banned from the airwaves on the grounds that they would be "harmed" by Collin's appearance on television. A lower court actually enjoined the broadcast of the program, but a higher court almost immediately lifted that ban. Had the ban stayed in effect, it would have put the proponents of menticide in the awkward position of insisting that they were not really damaging the First Amendment while that damage was present for all to see. Later, when NBC aired the television movie "Holocaust," even Abbott Rosen stopped insisting that menticide could not be used to censor beyond Skokie, for in that movie the perpetrators of menticide were everywhere.

Goldstein v. *Collins* was created and filed in panic; it was built upon a foundation of seriously flawed principles, which were indisputably subject to misuse. In spite of the desperation which those facts exemplify, they do not suggest the totality. To those considerable problems, Sol Goldstein added pure hypocrisy. In his willingness to help stop Frank Collin, Goldstein was willing to engage in intellectual fraud.

While Sol Goldstein argued before a court of law that he

had to be protected from Frank Collin's demonstrations lest he be seriously damaged, Sol Goldstein had in fact already witnessed Frank Collin demonstrating in uniform, and he had done so voluntarily. Before he came to the courts of Illinois begging protection from Frank Collin, Sol Goldstein had gone well out of his way to watch Collin demonstrate in Marquette Park.

Goldstein told David Goldberger — in a deposition taken as part of the preparation for a possible hearing in the suit — that he had gone to see Collin in Marquette Park months before Collin had even announced his plans for Skokie. That fact, whatever it indicates about Goldstein's sincere resolve to confront Frank Collin, made Sol Goldstein's presence in the litigation its most troubling aspect.

Even ignoring the remarkable fact that Goldstein was asking a court to prevent something that had already occurred with Goldstein's willing participation, the admission made the case impossibly weak. If menticide in fact exists and if it can in fact be proven to be a tort, the most sensible way to accomplish a legal victory over it would be to prove that it had occurred and sue for damages. Goldstein, assuming the theory as he wanted it applied, had already suffered menticide when he came before the court. Instead of asking the court to punish Frank Collin for a tort which could be proved to have occurred, however, Goldstein asked the court to prevent a future tort. Where he might have successfully sued Collin for the damage inflicted, he rather asked for unconstitutional relief against future conduct. At a legal level, Goldstein's strategy was sheer folly; at a logical level, it left gaping holes.

The reason — the all too obvious reason — for Goldstein's odd request of the court was clear: he could not sue Collin for menticide which occurred in Marquette Park because he had witnessed the demonstration of his own free will. Collin could not be sued for forcing Goldstein to come to Marquette Park, because he had not done so; neither could he be sued for directly confronting Goldstein with his hatred by going after Goldstein, because he had not done that either. If menticide had occurred, in short, Sol Goldstein was just as responsible for it as Frank Collin was.

For precisely that reason, of course, Goldstein's plea for a ban on Collin's demonstration was equally empty. Anyone who went to see Frank Collin in Skokie would do so because they *wanted* to; if they were harmed by their own action — the action of going to see Collin — when it combined with Collin's actions, both were equally responsible for the harm.

Jerome Torshen usually responded to that line of reasoning by insisting that a survivor who witnessed a Collin demonstration did not do so of free will; rather, he was *driven* by the torment of the memories to confront Collin. For a few survivors, that may well be true; for all survivors it cannot be true, for Sol Goldstein is probably the *only* member of the class he claimed to represent who actually went to Marquette Park — whether "driven" or otherwise — to confront Frank Collin. The few who can prove that they are compelled beyond control to see Frank Collin may be entitled to punitive damages when that proof can be made, but even Goldstein, the representative of the class, could not claim to have been drawn to Collin's demonstrations, for he had seen but one or two.

Founded on that confusing mass of ill-conceived notions,

the menticide theory was hardly the stuff of which the First Amendment is likely to be rewritten. As an instrument designed to gain public support, however, the Goldstein litigation was ideal. In the hands of a zealot like Jerome Torshen, the menticide theory became a dangerous weapon.

The emotional content of the survivor litigation was undeniably compelling. The suit sought to protect from further assault the victims of a lawless, wanton, horrid assault. That principle led Jerome Torshen to treat his lawsuit as a crusade in which the enemy was to be spared no attack. Where a sensitive, considerate appeal would have worked wonders, Torshen used a meat-ax.

Torshen's tactics seemed all the more dreadful because Harvey Schwartz, Skokie's lawyer, provided such a stunning contrast. When the law student at the University of Chicago attacked me, Harvey Schwartz had risen instantly to defend ACLU's role in the litigation; when members of an exclusively Jewish audience attacked ACLU, Torshen told them that he did not care what happened to his opponents.

While Schwartz maintained a professional, respectful relationship with Goldberger, Torshen behaved like a child. At one point in the proceedings, he actually filed with the court a document which called David Goldberger a "Neo-Nazi counsel." Torshen evidently wanted the court to believe that Goldberger was himself a Fascist; when Goldberger protested to Torshen, Torshen shrugged the matter off. Absolutely furious that Torshen had brought the personal attack into a court of law, I called both Abbott Rosen and Aryeh Neier, ACLU's national executive director.

Rosen listened and indicated his willingness to look into the matter. Neier roared when he heard the news, so thoroughly furious at the attack that he immediately called the national ADL office to demand an apology. At the next court hearing in the litigation, Jerome Torshen apologized for characterizing his fellow lawyer as a Neo-Nazi.

In public gatherings about the Skokie controversy, Jerome Torshen shamelessly used his clients. In order to win support for his point of view, Torshen would hammer away at audiences about the anguish and torment of the survivor community, linking salvation from that torment to his litigation. In the process, Torshen always somehow managed to imply that anyone who opposed his point of view was without feeling for, or incapable of understanding, the survivors' pain.

In the right forum, that linkage of the holocaust to Collin and hence to ACLU was devastating. In a private home, while I sat listening, Torshen set out that argument before an audience composed exclusively of Jews. As a non-Jew (and a blond, blue-eyed non-Jew at that), I was virtually defenseless against that attack. There was nothing I could say to a roomful of angry Jews which would convince them that I understood, and cared more deeply than ever about, the survivors. I left that particular gathering convinced that Jerry Torshen might be somewhat less shameless than he is cruel.

The survivor litigation, once it arrived in court, did not fare well. The actual theory of the litigation — and the remarkable machinations of both Sol Goldstein and Jerome Torshen — never came to trial at all.

When the suit was filed in mid-summer David Goldberger responded with a petition asking the court to dismiss the litigation. The petition noted that one injunction was already in effect against the demonstration and that two injunctions are not better than one; the petition also noted that whatever law came from the appeal of the Skokie litigation would govern this new suit as well, since both sought injunctive relief of precisely the same dimensions.

Before the matter of dismissing the suit could be argued, however, there was a preliminary matter to be dealt with. In Cook County, cases are assigned to specific judges by the chief judge within the proper division. When the Goldstein litigation came to the chancery court, it was promptly assigned to Judge Joseph Wosik. Since Judge Wosik had already issued one injunction against Frank Collin, it hardly seemed a proper assignment, although it was without doubt consistent with the bulk of the judicial conduct in the Skokie controversy. However, at the request of Frank Collin's counsel, the case was transferred to another court.

The motion to dismiss the suit against Collin was denied in the second court. At the same time, however, the court left open the possibility for another injunction in the future. As soon as the judge had denied the petition to dismiss the case, David Goldberger asked the judge to certify for an appeal his refusal to dismiss, indicating his desire to have the matter reviewed by a higher court. The judge agreed to the certification, and as soon as he did, David asked the court to delay the hearing on the merits of the survivor litigation until that appeal could be resolved. Torshen objected, but the court agreed.

As a result of all that legal maneuvering, the survivor litigation was reduced to a procedural question having nothing to do with the theory of the actual case. The question on appeal was simply whether the judge had acted properly or not in refusing to dismiss the suit. That question wandered through the appeals process at the same pace as Skokie's suit did; after it consumed all that time, the suit itself was dismissed yet again. Perhaps because it was a redundancy or perhaps because it was a legal thicket far too perplexing to even consider, the Goldstein litigation ultimately served nobody, least of all the Jewish community it was intended to serve.

6

Sticks and Stones

The second significant path which the Jewish community's response to the Skokie controversy followed was markedly more direct — and surely a lot more satisfying — than the perplexing menticide theory. In protest of ACLU's role in the Skokie controversy, Jewish members of ACLU began to resign.

The letters of resignation started, in a trickle, almost as soon as the controversy itself became public. They built at a steady pace through the summer and well into the fall. Although we felt at the time that it was not appropriate to emphasize the fact (lest we still further offend the Jewish community), the vast majority of the letters of resignation came from members who identified themselves as Jews.

The arguments contained in the letters of resignation paralleled, with remarkable regularity, the arguments that David, a few other speakers, and I encountered in virtually every public forum on the topic. The people who argued against us fell into two broad groups: those who believed that we were misinterpreting in some way the First Amendment and those who refused to support us, regardless of the position we took, because Collin was the client. Without exception, the arguments used could not overcome the principal difficulty that Skokie's lawyers faced in the courts: in order to get to Frank Collin, it was necessary to

go through the First Amendment. In the particular circumstances of the controversy, there was simply no way over,
under, or around the doctrine of free speech.

By far, the argument which most appeared in the letters
of resignation and on the speaking circuit as well was based
on the doctrine of "falsely shouting 'FIRE' in a crowded
theater." It is clearly an exception to the First Amendment
with which most people are at least passingly familiar; I
never spoke to an audience which did not raise the "Fire"
doctrine.

As popular as it was, the doctrine as drawn by the Supreme Court had absolutely no applicability to the Skokie
controversy or to the demonstration contemplated in the
village. Even ignoring the elements of the doctrine itself,
"Fire" is a *post*-speech doctrine, one intended not for
prior restraint but for after-the-fact law. Even if it had fit
the Skokie controversy, it would have been useful only
after Frank Collin had demonstrated, at which time it
could have been used to strike down Collin's First Amendment defense ("The First Amendment does not apply to
this speech, your Honor, because the speech falls under the
'Fire' exception to free speech"). While it is probably illegal to shout "Fire" in a crowded theater, it is not illegal
to think about doing so.

Even though the doctrine does not apply in prior
restraint circumstances, it was certainly put forward in
that context. Although the protesters insisted, even to the
point of withdrawing support from ACLU, that "Fire"
applied to Skokie, the doctrine simply did not fit. Several
elements which are required for the doctrine to work are
just not present in the Skokie circumstances, chief among
them the "crowded theater" itself.

120

The doctrine contemplates a captive audience, one which is confined (inside the theater) and unable to escape the shout. Since Collin's proposed demonstration was to be out of doors, confinement could not exist, for anyone wishing to escape the shout could simply walk away from it.

The "theater" element of the doctrine also contemplates another critical circumstance: surprise. Those assembled in the theater are there expecting a particular message or communication (a play, a movie, a speech). They are not only unable to escape the message, they are also surprised by it. The surprise, in turn, causes panic. Since the greater part of the English-speaking world was clearly going to know about Frank Collin's Skokie demonstration in advance, the element of surprise could not exist. If the surprise is not present, neither is the panic, and panic is the most critical element of the doctrine.

In the panic which would follow a dramatic, unexpected communication such as a shout of "Fire," further communication would be prevented. It is that *censorship* which the Supreme Court used as the basis for the entire doctrine, for the other point of view ("Wait! There is no fire.") must be protected. It is for that reason that the doctrine contemplates a *false* shout; the error automatically gives rise to a second point of view. Since the Village of Skokie had given absolutely no indication of a willingness to censor other points of view intentionally, the doctrine of falsely shouting "Fire" in a crowded theater simply did not apply. Whatever Frank Collin shouted, it would not prevent the communication of a different point of view. Those who doubted that another point of view would be heard needed only to be reminded that, on the one occasion when Collin had been thought to be heading for Skokie, thousands of his detractors had been waiting to communicate.

When "Fire" wasn't cited, incitement to riot was. A surprising number of resignees argued that Frank Collin would incite a riot if he went to Skokie, and most audiences raised that argument or one much like it as well. But despite its apparent validity, it fits the circumstances no more effectively than the "Fire" argument does.

Incitement to riot is a specific criminal charge. The crime occurs when somebody urges upon an audience unlawful conduct which the audience then undertakes to commit. It is, again, a post-speech action: after the speaker has spoken and after the audience has acted, the speaker is arrested for inciting the audience. It is not possible to arrest anyone for incitement to riot unless the riot has occurred.

Wholly apart from the absence of any relationship to prior restraint, incitement also clashes with common sense. Given the opposition which he generated even without setting foot in Skokie, it is difficult to imagine what Collin could say to the audience there with which they would be willing to agree. There is but one statement which Collin could make which would urge unlawful conduct upon the audience which the audience would be willing to undertake: if Frank Collin solicited a physical attack against himself, in Skokie, it seems likely that the audience would respond affirmatively. Short of that improbable request there is probably nothing which Collin could urge upon Skokie's citizens which they would be willing to consider. If he cannot persuade them to riot, he cannot be charged with incitement.

Although the form of the incitement to riot theory sometimes changed slightly — sometimes it would appear as "disorderly conduct," sometimes as "Collin will provoke an attack" — it always led to a broader discussion. By raising the question of incitement, ACLU's critics and resignees struck at the most critical distinction of all, the vast distinction, in law, between words and actions. There is a line, defined as precisely as possible by the laws of incitement, beyond which speech is not protected by the First Amendment. It is the line between advocacy and action.

The difference between advocacy and action is better described by a children's rhyme than by lawyers and case law: "Sticks and stones may break my bones, but names will never hurt me." The rhyme is perfectly consistent with the First Amendment, for no word ever committed a crime, no name ever violated a law, no speech ever broke a bone. While the idea may be criminal upon implementation, the idea itself is not criminal.

Frank Collin's doctrine is monstrous and evil. If it were implemented, it would instantly generate criminal activity. If Collin could find an audience willing to begin the implementation of his platform, he would surely be subject to criminal charges and a trial. The use of the sticks and stones of fascism, however, is far different from the use of the names of fascism, for the mere uttering of an idea, without action, is not a crime.

Neither is an idea obscene, although many critics argued that Collin could be censored on the grounds of obscenity. While it is hardly an overstatement to say that Collin's doctrine is obscene, that moral judgment cannot be translated into a legal one. The law governing obscenity in

123

America has always been confined to sexually oriented *material*. No idea — and certainly no political idea — has ever been adjudged obscene. That firm legal stand is not only consistent with the First Amendment, it is, because of its consistency, eminently sensible as well. There is no doubt that an opening of the obscenity floodgates to political dialogue in America would lead to wholesale censorship. Abortion advocates and foes would surely insist that each was obscene, and there is little doubt about what the antihomosexual forces of America would do with such power. It is equally hard to imagine the most freedom-loving liberal resisting the chance to use obscenity charges against Richard Nixon.

A significant number of the members who resigned — matched again by large numbers of people in the audiences I addressed — did not care about ACLU's reading of the First Amendment. In two forms, however, they objected strenuously to ACLU's participation. Either they refused to let their money be used to defend Collin, or they argued that ACLU had no business defending somebody who would destroy basic rights if he came to power. In either form, the question was essentially the same: "How can an organization which is supposed to defend rights work for somebody who would eradicate them?"

Over the course of the public encounters, I grew accustomed to the snickers that accompanied my response to that question; the snickers were the embarrassed (or, perhaps, cynical) response to my profession of faith in American democracy. However out of fashion that may be, it is nevertheless the only answer which can be given.

The unpleasant fact is that Frank Collin's rights are

those of a citizen of the United States, which is to say that they are the rights of everyone. If Collin does not have them, nobody does, for there is no available method of revoking Collin's right to speak without revoking the rights of others as well. So long as that is true, any assault on Collin's right to speak is an assault on someone else's right to speak. Skokie had effectively censored Collin with their permit/insurance ordinance, but the Jewish War Veterans had been censored by the same device. Any method of censoring an unpopular idea can be used to censor other unpopular ideas, until we discover that there is, in fact, no substantive difference between the legal argument (heckler's veto) which Skokie used to stop Collin and the legal argument (again, the heckler's veto) which was used to attempt to prevent Martin Luther King, Jr., from marching on Selma, Alabama.

In both instances, the audience reaction to the expression of an idea was put forth as grounds for censoring the idea. That is not to say that Collin and King are comparable, an accusation that I grew more than tired of hearing, but it is intended to suggest that both exercise exactly the same right. If ACLU fails to protect the First Amendment from the assault upon Collin, where will the same argument next arise? In a busing controversy in which one side threatens to attack the other? In a heated union dispute?

The First Amendment protects all ideas, including Frank Collin's ideas, because that protection is the life, the essential element, of democracy itself. The guarantee the First Amendment provides is the guarantee upon which rests the right of the people to govern themselves. From *all* available ideas, the citizens of this country select those with which they are in agreement and reject those with which they disagree. That selection is not made for once and for all, it is made every day and shifts as the political spectrum of ideas itself shifts.

The argument which held that protecting Collin's right to demonstrate in Skokie is a waste of the resources of a civil-liberties organization was, by far, the most depressing of all those raised against us. Those who argued that Frank Collin should not have rights or that Frank Collin with rights will destroy the rights of others expressed, in their arguments, an absolute lack of faith in the wisdom of the body politic. They implied — and an astonishing number seemed to actually believe — that Collin could gain support for his doctrine if and when he aired it.

That fear is the risk which comes with democracy itself. There will always be "bad" ideas, ideas which by their nature deserve instant rejection. Frank Collin's ideas fall within that category, a fact which could not have been made more clear by the very reactions of those who knew of the controversy. The only sure way to reject such ideas is to examine them fully, to attack them for their flaws, to reject them for their inhumanity, and the only way to examine, attack, or reject ideas is to listen to them first. Even before the controversy had a full discussion, the rejection was taking place; it was taking place because there was ample debate — ample *speech* — taking place.

Eventually, most of the argument over the principles of democracy involved in the Skokie controversy came down to a single, dramatic confrontation — a confrontation in which somebody (more often than not a survivor or an individual who cited the survivors) would say, directly,

"It *can* happen here." More often than not, such an assertion would be preceded by the recitation of one or more real or imagined parallels between the United States and pre-war Germany ("look at the inflation," "look at the crime wave," "this is exactly how Hitler started").

I sometimes felt the need to apologize for my reply, but the reply itself did not vary: I do not believe for one moment that the citizens of this nation would tolerate for a single moment anything faintly related to the implementation of Frank Collin's doctrine. If and when such an event occurs, I will be among those leading the revolution which will have become absolutely necessary; until then, I insist that we are, as a people, far too wise to accept what Frank Collin offers. I regret, if anything, that I apologized to anyone for that belief.

The legal portion of the Skokie controversy was ready for resolution in the fall of 1977. There was, however, no rush to judgment. No court would rule on the substantive issues of the dispute until well after the first of the New Year.

The injunction, still standing, was before the Illinois Supreme Court, where in September it was fully argued and "briefed." ("Brief" is, of course, the perfect legal contradiction — no lawyer's "brief" ever is.)

The three ordinances were challenged, in federal district court, soon after the summer ended. In a case brought on behalf of Frank Collin, ACLU sought to have each of the three ordinances struck down as unconstitutional. By mid-fall, the largely paper case was before the court for adjudication.

The menticide litigation was mired in the appeals process. Eventually, the question of whether to dismiss that suit or not worked its way up to the Illinois Supreme Court. Since the court was already sitting on the substantive question of an actual injunction, it was assumed that the ruling on Skokie's injunction would almost surely govern the injunction sought by the survivors as well.

From the middle of the summer, when the Illinois Appellate Court had modified, once again, the original injunction until the last days of January 1978, when the supreme court ruled on the appeal, the only judicial action even remotely related to Skokie was the brief moment of censorship in Philadelphia.

The old litigation challenging the Chicago Park District's quarter-million-dollar insurance requirement also languished through the fall and winter, a fact which nobody, at the time, thought momentous. When the courts finally began to rule, the insurance suit would become completely entangled in the Skokie controversy. Since not even Frank Collin knew that the entanglement would take place, however, hardly anyone even noticed the insurance suit.

As the courts sat in quiet deliberation, the battle outside raged on.

The press continued to devote attention to the controversy. In the absence of any hard legal news, the media was content to explore the broader aspects of the issues. Newspapers editorialized anew on the issues, television reports analyzed the roots of the survivors' anguish or offered interviews with one or more of the participants in the controversy, and national columnists continued to take sides on the questions. William F. Buckley, Jr., won the office award for novelty; he opposed the demonstration on grounds that it would constitute heresy.

The hellish pace of speaking engagements continued

without letup; if anything, the opening of schools created a still larger demand for ACLU speakers. A handful of board members were by now handling some of the requests, and among them they usually took on about a quarter of the total; David and I took the remaining engagements ourselves.

After a summer full of public encounters, the speaking engagements began to take on an odd character: they were at once dreadfully boring and tensely exhilarating. The boredom came of the content of the debate itself, a debate in which the arguments quite literally never changed or varied at all. It was "FIRE" and "incitement" and "Fascists have no rights" and "what about the survivors" over and over again.

However predictable the content of the arguments, the energy and passion which each new audience would bring to the debate was equally so. In each new forum, the audience was angry and aggressive and highly emotional, and no matter how easy it became to recite the responses to the arguments, it was never easy to reply to the emotional issues. Each new encounter required that the audience's passion and energy be matched, and in many encounters there was the possibility that somebody would get too emotional or too angry. It became a fatiguing circuit to travel by the middle of the fall.

Eventually, only drama or humor would make any given encounter stand out. On a university campus, the local police came up with the least expensive deterrent to crime I had ever seen. As a routine matter, David and I now requested that basic security precautions be taken by the sponsors of large gatherings; in response to that request the university police simply parked an empty cruiser in front of the building where I spoke. I do not believe that an officer was assigned to that cruiser, although the presence of an officer was certainly implied, so that the department had evidently turned an unused vehicle into a crime-stopper.

At the other end of the spectrum, a sizable audience of students at the University of Wisconsin listened as a member of a group known as the Committee Against Racism (they were the folks who had staged a sit-in at our office in Chicago during the summer) called upon "the people" to come to Skokie and physically attack Frank Collin and anyone supporting him. When the students heard the end of the proviolence speech, fully half of them applauded loudly, shouting support.

Considerably more subtle exchanges also stood out from the routine on occasion. I could not decide, and ultimately gave up trying to decide, whether to laugh or cry about the predicament involving rabbis which I often faced. In many of the Jewish gatherings I faced, the congregation's rabbi would be present in the room. I would give my view of the law governing free speech, and, at some point thereafter, the rabbi would offer a contrary view. As the literal "giver of laws" for his congregation, the rabbi never failed to persuade the audience of the fallacy of my reasoning.

A somewhat less subtle exchange with a rabbi also stood out during the long period of court deliberation. At a gathering of Jews at a community center in Skokie, a young rabbi included in his presentation a personal, harsh attack on David Goldberger as a Jew. I was not qualified to reply (nor did I think the topic appropriate in any event), so I let it go with a passing reference. Two or three weeks later, in another forum, the same rabbi shared a panel table with me. This time, I asked him in advance to refrain from launching a personal attack on Goldberger until such time as David could respond in person. The rabbi nodded and, twenty minutes later, launched the same attack almost word for word.

David encountered such hatred firsthand, of course, in nearly every forum at which he appeared. A routine speaking engagement for David included at least one personal attack; the highlights for David became a sustained audience disruption or an overt physical threat.

For all of the energy they demanded and all of the emotional responses they exacted, the speaking engagements were still far more pleasant than the work required in the office. By October, it was clear that the membership damage to ACLU (across the country, but particularly in Illinois) was going to be very, very high, and as difficult as the speeches became, they never matched the discomfort of watching the budget erode as the staff wondered who, by January, would still be around.

We had labored, through the summer, without any solid information about our membership income. As usual the national membership department was trying to find (never mind operate) its computer, so it was not until the middle of October that we got our first reports of the summer's membership activity. We had lost at least six hundred members in just over four months.

Astonished, I called the membership office to confirm the figures our computer report offered. The call resulted not only in a confirmation of the figures, it provided hard proof. Most of the letters of resignation had, it turned out, gone to the national office, where they had accumulated until I finally called. Then, and only then, did the membership staff get around to forwarding the more than six hundred letters of resignation to me.

With those early figures, I began to work on the coming year's budget. We were, at that moment, in the heart of both our annual ACLU membership renewal campaign and our annual Roger Baldwin Foundation fund-raising efforts (the foundation is the actual litigation agency, separate from ACLU yet sharing the same basic goals); the two efforts combined to generate virtually all of our income. Based on what we already knew about the membership losses, our projections for the coming year were grim indeed.

We watched, through November and into December, as the losses mounted up. We projected, at a minimum, losses of at least 30 percent of our total income. On my recommendation, just as the year drew to a close, the board approved a budget in which three staff positions had been eliminated and two others had been reduced to half-time; in all, five of our thirteen employees were gone by the first of the year.

The tension and anxiety in our office throughout this period was significant naturally; for the first time, however, real bitterness began to surface as well. For one thing, David and I both knew full well that the Anti-Defamation League, faced with exactly the same dilemma of principle which we confronted, had deserted theirs; while we slashed our staff, the ADL continued business as usual. It was virtually impossible not to resent that fact.

Others on the ACLU staff reacted in differen, ways. One member, the most junior member of the staff, took to telling everyone how to run the office, becoming nearly insufferable in the process. A senior staff member, evidently convinced that my board-approved budget was based on faulty figures, solicited and got a secret meeting with members of the board. When I learned of the session, dead in the center of the grim budgetary process, I saw it as a double betrayal. I was fully prepared to fire this person on the spot for going around me to the board and ready to scream at the board for letting her. David prevailed upon me to ignore the incident.

So we came to the end of the year. In the eight months of the controversy, the world had turned inside out. Our faith in the supremacy of the First Amendment and the system of freedom it supports had been met in public with open derision and in court with contrary judgment. Our members, who had never before reacted so suddenly to anything ACLU had done in its fifty-year existence, were leaving in droves, taking their financial support with them. Our colleagues in the office were either cleaning out their desks or preparing to take on additional work for which there would be little if any additional compensation. In the exact same period of time Frank Collin — the racist, the Fascist, the ultimate American enemy — had enjoyed national media attention and ever increasing notoriety; he had, in short, not been damaged in any way at all, save by the exposure of opposition to him which had, after all, never gone away. It all seemed, somehow, upside-down.

7

"One Man's Lyric"

The case of *Village of Skokie* v. *Frank Collin* was decided, on January 27, 1978, by the Illinois Supreme Court: "We accordingly, albeit reluctantly, conclude that the display of the swastika cannot be enjoined under the fighting-words exception to free speech, nor can anticipation of a hostile audience justify the prior restraint."

The state supreme court found, nine months after it had been issued, that the injunction preventing Frank Collin's proposed demonstration in the village was completely, thoroughly, entirely unconstitutional. Each of the arguments raised in opposition to the demonstration — by the village's lawyers, by the survivor litigation, and by ACLU's legion of critics — was rejected, and the total defense against the demonstration was dealt a mortal blow.

The village's lawyers had argued, before the appellate court, that the display of the swastika in Skokie would constitute "fighting words" and would therefore justify prior restraint. The court held that the display itself did not, in fact, constitute "fighting words" and went beyond that argument to the issue of the display of the swastika before Skokie's unique audience: "We do not doubt that the sight of this symbol is abhorrent to the Jewish citizens of Skokie, and that the survivors of the Nazi persecution, tormented by their recollections, may have strong feelings

135

regarding its display. Yet it is entirely clear that this factor does not justify enjoining defendants' speech."

The village's lawyers had argued for a "heckler's veto," for a halt to the demonstration on the grounds that the audience might become lawless. The court held that such lawlessness could not be attributed to the speaker, for "a speaker who gives prior notice of his message has not compelled a confrontation with those who voluntarily listen." Although Skokie's lawyers argued that the courts must protect the audience (and the survivors' position was that the audience would actually be harmed), the court found in that position no justification for halting Collin, rather placing "the burden on the viewer to avoid further bombardment."

Skokie's litigation and the survivor litigation as well had implied that the monstrosity of Collin's particular doctrine was enough to support the prior restraint. The court responded that all ideas are protected by the First Amendment, that "one man's vulgarity is another's lyric."

Technically, the Illinois Supreme Court held that the appeals court had properly struck down all of the original injunction except the swastika ban. The supreme court itself then struck down that last remaining portion of the injunction, rendering the entire ban on Collin's demonstration void. At the same time, without additional opinion, the supreme court dismissed the survivor suit, *Goldstein* v. *Collin.* There seemed no reason for either more hearings on that suit or any additional language from the court about it, since the suit had sought an injunction precisely like the one just held unconstitutional in the Skokie suit.

The news of the supreme court's ruling broke on a

Friday afternoon, and the brief lull in constant press attention to the story — a respite which had begun in the middle
of November — ended immediately. The ruling itself and
the reactions to it by the various participants in the controversy dominated news in Chicago throughout the
weekend; through wire services and electronic coverage,
the story received national attention as well.

Among the various reactions to the story there were
enough surprises to keep the press very busy. For one
thing, Frank Collin was nowhere to be found. It turned
out that Collin was stuck in a snowstorm somewhere
between St. Louis and Chicago when the supreme court
ruled. Although they tried their best (one reporter demanded angrily that I tell him where to find Collin,
insisting that I must be concealing the information), the
press could not, on this one occasion, include any of
Frank Collin's smug remarks in their stories.

Frank Collin's absence enhanced still another surprising
development in the overall controversy, for it seemed to
enhance the ambiguity with which Collin himself seemed
to view his plan to demonstrate in Skokie. Even when he
became available to the press, Collin did not announce a
new demonstration date; instead, he said he would wait
to see what the federal courts did in the case involving
Skokie's three ordinances. Although there were, at the
time, absolutely no barriers preventing Collin from at
least planning a demonstration, he elected not to do so.
That fact, along with the contents of a letter Collin had
sent to a Chicago paper before the supreme court had
ruled, seemed to suggest that somehow something had
changed.

Frank Collin's letter to the editors of the Chicago

Tribune, which was printed in the paper on January 11, contained a new rationale for the proposed demonstration in Skokie. Collin asserted that he had decided to demonstrate in Skokie because he was being locked out of Marquette Park by the Chicago Park District. He was coming to Skokie, the letter suggested, to dramatize the censorship in Chicago. The letter did not suggest a trade — one forum for the other — but that possibility clearly suggested itself. If Skokie was Collin's target because Marquette Park was not available, then Skokie would not be the target if the park were available.

Collin's letter and his subsequent failure to seize the opportunity to set a demonstration date in Skokie seemed to suggest that he was wavering. By January, Frank Collin had seen nine months of sustained fury over his plan. Even if he had not been the direct target of that fury all the time, he could not miss its depth. If nothing else, Collin knew that Sol Goldstein had faced him in a courtroom and all but threatened to attack him. The furor his plan had generated had also kicked off a call (from groups including anti-Fascist organizations and the JDL) for a direct physical confrontation in Skokie, or at least a call to give such a confrontation a healthy try.

Collin must also have understood that there was a strong likelihood of his arrest if and when he went to Skokie. He had been arrested in Chicago for merely appearing near the park, and if a large crowd in fact appeared with Collin in Skokie, the village's officials would probably wish their charge confined elsewhere than in the village itself. His arrest would likely land him in the Cook County Jail. A sprawling, often nearly lawless place which is packed to its walls, Cook County Jail is

138

populated overwhelmingly by black males. It is the sort of place likely to make Frank Collin wish for the comparative mercy of the JDL.

As mindful as he was of the physical danger he faced, Frank Collin was by January equally aware of the fact that he had won, in a federal court, the right to demonstrate in Marquette Park only to discover that the Chicago Park District was nevertheless willing to thwart his attempts to do so. As he saw the park district play fast and loose with his rights, Frank Collin was probably as frustrated as he was frightened.

In July 1977, U.S. District Court Judge George Leighton had handed down a preliminary order in Collin's challenge to the park district's insurance requirement. Leighton, persuaded of the strong likelihood that the requirement would, upon close examination, be found unconstitutional, ordered a temporary halt to its enforcement. In response, Frank Collin applied for a permit to demonstrate in Marquette Park.

The park district's response to Collin's application was something of a shock. Leighton had not ruled the insurance requirement out, the park district told Collin, only the dollar amount; therefore, Collin would be required to post sixty — rather than two hundred and fifty — thousand dollars of insurance.

Amazed, David Goldberger went back to Judge Leighton, where he argued, again, that there had been proof before the court that Collin could not obtain insurance in any amount and that any amount was therefore unlawful; moreover, David said, Leighton's own order said that the requirement itself was unlawful. Richard Troy, the park district's clever attorney, responded (perhaps already aware of Leighton's displeasure with his actions) that perhaps there had been a misunderstanding and, in any event, the date for which Collin had applied was not available. If Collin would reapply, Troy said, everything would be cleared up.

"Everything" cleverly excluded the park itself. By the time Richard Troy had danced his way around the preliminary order and back into the courtroom, the weather had accomplished what Troy's litigation could not: it was too cold and snowy to demonstrate in Marquette Park.

Although he had won the right to do so in July, Collin had been unable to demonstrate in Marquette Park ever since. That frustration, playing against his legitimate fears of a confrontation in Skokie, had caused Frank Collin to back away from his plan to demonstrate in Skokie.

Ironically, Collin's shift of attention away from Skokie came at exactly the time Skokie's officials seemed to resign themselves to Collin's eventual presence. The village's lawyers and elected officials had one more appeal available; they could go directly from the Illinois Supreme Court to the United States Supreme Court. When the state court ruled, the anticipated "we'll fight to the finish" announcement of an appeal did not come. Instead, the village's officials, like Collin, pronounced themselves content to wait for the ruling of the federal court on the three ordinances.

The failure to take an immediate appeal to the U.S. Supreme Court signaled, if not resignation, a less aggressive posture on the part of the village. As dramatic as that shift seemed to be, it was not without justification.

The initial reaction among the village leaders to Collin's

plan had been to let it happen. They had not been able to persuade their constituency of the wisdom of that plan; rather, the roar of opposition to Collin's demonstration had forced the village to go to court. While some of the village's officials (notably Mayor Albert Smith) had taken a very aggressive stand in support of the litigation, others had expressed public doubts. In particular, Skokie's legal counsel, Harvey Schwartz, seemed to understand that the village stood on very shaky legal ground. Although he never failed to defend his litigation thoroughly in public debates, Schwartz usually agreed that ACLU had raised legitimate, if not compelling, arguments on the other side.

Those who had doubts about the wisdom of the legal position were hardly comforted by the supreme court ruling, of course. However aggressive the village might want to be, it was now evident that the courts were not prepared to respond favorably any longer. That reason alone may have been enough to soften Skokie's position, although there were other just as compelling reasons everywhere the village officials looked.

For one thing, the impact of the legal battle on Skokie's residents had been anything but salutary. After nine months of litigation which had caused sustained turmoil and emotional tension, the village's officials had nothing to show for their efforts but the prospect of still more turmoil and tension. The longer the village stayed in court fighting, the longer its Jewish population would remain tense and angry and threatened.

The village's officials, moreover, could take no solace from the impact the controversy born of their litigation seemed to be having on their own image. For one thing, the litigation had become the vehicle that Frank Collin rode to national prominence, and it was certainly clear by January that Collin would enjoy that notoriety for as long as the controversy remained alive. However unwittingly, Skokie was keeping Frank Collin in the news.

At the same time, of course, Skokie was keeping itself in the news, for the glare of media attention focused on the village just as intensely as on Collin. The village's officials found their community constantly in the news, always as the place where the Nazis wanted to march, and usually as the place where the censorship was taking place. Wholly apart from the drain on their energies exacted by the coverage, Skokie's officials found that the press coverage itself was not doing the image of the community much good.

A grim turn of events, absolutely unrelated to the Nazi controversy, had also damaged the village's reputation. Two murder victims, both apparently killed elsewhere, were dumped in Skokie during the winter. Reeling from the controversial news of the dispute and shocked by the crimes, Skokie's officials retained a public relations counselor. (Harvey Schwartz, at the time, told me that *he* thought the public relations firm retained by the village should confine its efforts to keeping murderers from unloading their victims' bodies within the village limits; he may have been the only village official with a sense of humor left by then.)

For all of those reasons, and out of a desire to get the entire matter over and done with, Skokie's officials responded to the court's ruling with decided reserve.

In the offices of the American Civil Liberties Union in Chicago, the decision of the Illinois Supreme Court was greeted with a nearly audible sigh of relief. After nine perfectly dismal months of sustained criticism and severe damage, the position that had caused both was vindicated. All of Skokie's legal arguments — those directly related to the injunction as well as those related more directly to the ordinances — had been soundly rejected; in the process, each of ACLU's painfully held positions was ratified. At each new turn in the wake of the decision, we found new confidence.

The texture of the public debate changed instantly. Where David and I and the others speaking about the controversy had put forth our position as the way the law *should* be, we now argued our position as the law actually was. No longer did ACLU alone say Collin had the right to march — now the law said it, just as eloquently and with full judicial force. Those of our critics who still held to their positions were now in the position of arguing against the highest court in Illinois; with no little satisfaction, David and I happily stood aside while critics attacked the court instead of us.

The confidence generated by the supreme court's decision quickly surfaced. At the national level, ACLU's leaders took the court's affirmation as the logical beginning point for a new, positive effort to repair the damage sustained during the fall. Moving quickly, the national staff began to plan for a First Amendment Convocation at which ACLU would, presumably, proudly exhibit its willingness to defend even the most unpopular speakers, supported by the law; at the same time, the convocation would become a device with which to raise funds to offset the membership losses.

Simultaneously, ACLU's national leadership began to

plan for an internal campaign aimed at securing an extra contribution from the members who had not resigned. That campaign, like the call to the convocation, would be based on the assertion that ACLU had done its job all along (and done it well, by the court's measure) and that the organization should not die for that effort.

For all the support the supreme court decision provided, both practical and principled, our public reaction to it was nearly as muted as the village's had been. We expressed our satisfaction, real as it was, quietly and subtly. We told the reporters that we were very gratified at the decision on behalf of our real client (the First Amendment), but we also noted that the consequences of the victory for freedom of speech were not to our liking.

Since one result of our work in support of free speech was to increase the potential for painful anguish among all Jews and Skokie's Jews in particular, David and I had long ago learned that no victory in this litigation would merit the language of celebration. We had seen firsthand more than enough of the anguish of Frank Collin's targets to applaud still more of it.

Still, there was ample room for quiet satisfaction in the ringing affirmation we had secured. Nobody took a greater share of that satisfaction (or used it more effectively) than David Goldberger; but, then, nobody deserved it more. David's faith in both the supremacy of the First Amendment and the rule of law had been deeply shaken through the nine months of litigation prior to the court's ruling; the attacks upon him as a Jew had wounded David gravely; as a lawyer, David viewed the entire controversy in a more narrowly focused frame — for all of those reasons, David needed, and took, enormous strength from the ruling of the court.

My own view of the ruling was tempered considerably by circumstances other than those David faced. The decision came in the wake of the staff reductions, while I was still trying to figure out how to make the office run and enjoy the running of it without the good people who had left. In order to be free to run the litigation and ACLU's docket, David had by our mutual agreement remained as apart as possible from the process of paring back the staff. The process of reducing the staff—which I had believed to be one of the best among ACLU—came as I also endured an inordinate amount of travel. By the time the court ruled, I was far more tired than satisfied.

That disparity of reactions surprised neither David nor me, for we had spent the entire controversy supporting each other through the tribulations of it. I was used to sitting, behind the closed door of David's office, as he expressed his sometimes utter dismay at the mess we were in; he, in turn, had become accustomed to listening as I cursed the same mess. So I was not surprised to find that David was up when I was down. I was amazed, however, at the results of that particular disparity. David turned his confidence, born of the affirmation from the court, into a remarkable public appearance, which eventually kicked off a wave of support for ACLU.

Within days of the Illinois Supreme Court ruling, David taped a segment of the *Donahue* show. David arrived at the studio in blissful ignorance; he had no idea that the audience in the studio was almost entirely composed of Jews from Skokie, and he had no idea at all that the *Donahue* program runs, for nearly six weeks after it is taped, in something over one hundred and fifty cities. The audience in the studio was just as hostile as the audience beyond was enormous.

It was the sort of encounter upon which Phil Donahue's reputation has been built: very lively, extremely informative, and intensely personal. David, seated alone on the stage, faced an audience of very hostile critics. For an hour, he responded with quiet determination to all they offered, combining the confidence he took from the recent affirmative ruling with his own very real empathetic anguish about the plight of Collin's targets. David was, by all accounts, inspirational.

The *Donahue* show does not end — it echoes. For weeks after the program was taped the show was on the air somewhere. From the moment David returned to his office until the last airing had taken place well over a month later, the staff in ACLU's Chicago office enjoyed something we had not yet experienced: David Goldberger had tapped widespread support.

There were hundreds of letters of support for ACLU's position in the wake of the Donahue program. There were also letters of criticism and hatred (and an occasional proposition for David), but for the first time David received, and we all joined in, overwhelming expressions of support.

Thus renewed, we joined Collin and Skokie to wait for the next decision.

On February 23, 1978, United States District Court Judge Bernard Decker said, in his ruling on the three ordinances passed by the village, "It must be made clear from the outset that defendants [Skokie] have no power to prevent plaintiffs [Frank Collin] from stating their political philosophy, including their opinions of black and Jewish people, however noxious and reprehensible that philosophy may be. The Supreme Court has held that 'above all else, the First Amendment means that government has no power to restrict expression because of its message, its ideas, its subject matter, or its content.' "

Judge Decker found all three ordinances to be in violation of the U.S. Supreme Court's dictate. Although Decker created a procedural battle royal with his ruling, the substance of his opinion caused no significant battle at all. As the Illinois Supreme Court had done before him, Judge Decker laid out the law governing Collin's proposed demonstration in such rigid, fully documented language that Skokie's position was simply destroyed.

The first ordinance — which required insurance for street demonstrations, tied the insurance to a permit, and gave the village officials the power to waive those requirements at their own discretion — fell of its own weight. Judge Decker relied upon the previous rulings on the question of insurance in Chicago's parks. He noted that Judge Leighton (Decker's fellow jurist in the district court and the judge sitting on the Chicago Park District insurance litigation) had found the insurance scheme unconstitutional. He found Skokie's scheme equally so, noting that the insurance was probably not available to Collin at all, that Collin therefore would never be able to march or demonstrate in Skokie, and that others wishing to demonstrate there would simply win a waiver from sympathetic village officials. Decker found the entire scheme to be "covert censorship," and he struck down the whole ordinance, save only the requirement for thirty days' notice of a demonstration.

147

Decker swiftly disposed of the ordinance banning the use of "military style" uniforms in political demonstrations. Decker said, "It is obvious that this ordinance is directed specifically at Nazi uniforms and regalia. If Skokie really meant to enforce the ordinance as written, it would prohibit, among other things, an appearance by members of the American Legion in support of the candidates of the Democratic or Republican party." He found that the use of "distinctive clothing" as an expression of an idea is protected by the First Amendment and declared the ordinance void.

Judge Decker also found the village ordinance banning the dissemination of literature engaging in group libel to be unconstitutional, although in doing so he created a brief legal donnybrook. Decker ruled that the ordinance (which made the distribution of literature engaging in incitement to violence, hatred, or personal abuse illegal) was vague, overbroad, and inconsistent with existing First Amendment law.

Decker defined "vague" as the failure to communicate, in advance, the nature of the offense to be committed. He suggested that it would be impossible to know what, if any, statements might violate the ordinance. He noted that Frank Collin professes to be opposed to busing for racial integration of schools, suggesting that such a position might easily run afoul of the ordinance by seeming to be inciting "racial hatred." So long as Skokie could not define for Collin and everyone else the point at which the line between discussing busing and group libel would be crossed there could be no fair enforcement of the law; and, in the absence of fair enforcement, Decker ruled, that law must be struck.

The finding that Skokie's group libel ordinance was invalid caused a procedural problem that was composed of equal parts protocol and law. In finding the ordinance unconstitutional, Judge Decker had to confront a very old United States Supreme Court ruling on the question of group libel, a ruling that seemed to direct Decker in the opposite direction from the one he had chosen.

The case creating the problem was *Beauharnais v. Illinois,* which was decided by the United States Supreme Court in 1952. The Court had upheld the conviction of one Mr. Beauharnais, who had been convicted of violating an Illinois law that made group libel a crime. The case turned out to be one of those odd Supreme Court decisions that lost currency almost as soon as it was handed down. By the time Judge Decker ruled in 1978, he could fairly say that the case of Beauharnais had been "expressly over-ruled." It had not, however, been directly overruled and therein lay the problem.

In order to declare Skokie's libel ordinance unconstitutional, Decker had to appear to overrule a United States Supreme Court decision. As a district court judge, Decker had no such power. At the same time, Decker was evidently writing new law, an act which suggested that an appeal would be inevitable. Out of deference to the higher courts, then, and because Skokie surely wanted an appeal, Judge Decker declared the ordinance unconstitutional and stayed his own order for forty-five days, which left time, before the order took effect, for the appeal to go up to the Seventh Circuit Court of Appeals.

Judge Decker's ruling caused a sudden escalation in the tension of the controversy, but it caused another shift in the course of that controversy as well. Where

149

ACLU had been the target of the anger of the Jewish community, Frank Collin at last took his rightful place. When the courts began to use the power of the law to sweep away the barriers to Collin's village hall demonstration, the public perceptions began to change sharply.

It was no longer possible, for one thing, to criticize ACLU on grounds of misinterpretation of the law. The Illinois Supreme Court and Judge Decker had knocked down every argument that had been raised during the controversy (Judge Decker even dealt briefly with the notion that Collin is "obscene," a notion he flatly dismissed), and they had used virtually all of ACLU's arguments. While the ACLU's critics had no difficulty attacking the organization for its principles, it was not nearly so easy to attack the accumulated weight of the law.

The major shift occurred, however, because, with the rulings of the two courts, the prospect of an actual Nazi demonstration in Skokie became ever more real. As that prospect grew, the attention of ACLU's critics shifted away from ACLU and toward the more natural enemy, the man who would lead that demonstration.

Where there had been dozens of angry telephone calls to ACLU, there were now only a handful. Instead, the attention of our critics was directed at such matters as where, when, and under what circumstances to confront Frank Collin. Soon after Judge Decker's ruling was issued, Jewish organizations began to discuss plans for a massive counterdemonstration; if Frank Collin was going to come to Skokie, he would be met by hundreds, perhaps thousands, of citizens in opposition to his point of view.

Skokie's officials noticed the newest shift in the course of the controversy almost immediately. Soon after

Judge Decker had ruled (as local Jewish groups were tentatively calling for counterdemonstrations), Skokie's officials quietly responded to the shift by beginning to plan for what seemed the inevitable demonstrations.

Officials of the village made contact with the Community Relations Service of the U.S. Justice Department, seeking the assistance of that agency in planning for the coming confrontation. The CRS is an old agency within the Justice Department. It has no legal power at all but is supposed to assist in the mediation of public disputes arising out of legal confrontations. Under that broad mandate, CRS agents have served in school-busing disputes, civil-rights confrontations, and other such clashes, and now Skokie's officials wanted those same services. Two CRS agents, Richard Salem and Werner Petterson, were assigned to the case. On March 1, after preliminary discussion with Skokie's officials, both men came to ACLU's office to meet with David and me.

We took an instant dislike to both men. Their odd position in the dispute was as much the cause of that attitude as anything else, for in their constant assertions of "neutrality" they seemed to be willing to ignore the principles of free speech. We referred to the two men, more often than not, as "social workers," meaning (with derision intended) that they seemed to have no useful role in a legal dispute. Eventually, both Salem and Petterson would have a profound impact on the entire controversy — and a salutary one, at that — but in our early contact with them, as they continued to talk about dialogue, communication and expedition, they represented only the welcome fact that Skokie had, at last, begun to doubt the validity of its legal position.

151

The shift in the public focus on the controversy surfaced quickly, for by March 9 the organizers of the counter-demonstration were ready to go public. On that day, several Chicago-area Jewish organizations staged a press conference at which they announced their plans for, and issued a call to, a "massive confrontation" with Collin, if and when he appeared in Skokie.

Just as every new twist in the controversy now generated a new round of press accounts, so did that news conference. Between the substantial coverage the announcement received from the press and the grapevine communication system of the various Jewish groups, the reaction was swift and positive. Quickly, in New York and in Ohio and New Jersey and California, groups organized to come to Skokie, on notice, to demonstrate against Collin.

For all the coverage the press conference generated, none of it made reference to the dreadful irony that it exposed to the public. The principal spokesperson at the press conference, the man who said that he would lead the confrontation with Frank Collin, was Sol Goldstein. The man who had insisted (and who would insist again before the U.S. Supreme Court) that he would be harmed by a Neo-Nazi demonstration in Skokie was now calling upon citizens to stand beside him as he solicited the very harm he wanted the courts to prevent. Although there was a massive contradiction in his two positions, that fact went unreported.

Goldstein's seeming duplicity was probably the only aspect of the continuing controversy to go unreported during the wake of the two court rulings, for with those rulings the press had, if anything, increased the amount of attention given the story. In Chicago, the Skokie story had become a virtual day-to-day account, while, increasingly, the national media began to focus attention on the story as well. Indeed, by March I had grown accustomed to talking about the controversy with foreign journalists as well as national reporters. The Hong Kong *Morning Post* ran a front-page story about the confrontation; the Canadian Broadcast Corporation's reporters called so often that I came to know two of them by name.

In its extreme forms, the journalism which accompanied the court rulings and reactions during the winter of 1978 was the art at its worst. A wire-service reporter called Frank Collin's headquarters in the wake of the affirmative rulings to inquire about Collin's plans for a demonstration in Skokie. Collin was out when the call came, but one of his subordinates was all too willing to chatter away with a reporter. As a consequence, the reporter included in his story the suggestion — wholly unsupported by anything other than the remarks of the man on the phone at Frank Collin's number — that the National Socialist Party of America might demonstrate in Skokie on April 20, Adolf Hitler's birthday.

Frank Collin himself had no such plan. He had not provided Skokie's officials with notice of such a demonstration date; he had not announced to anyone else in the cast of the controversy his intention to stage such a demonstration. The idea was, at best, the musing speculation of a virtually unknown source. The story, in fact, did not generate much notice, because it did not appear in many outlets. It did appear, however, because all during March and well into April angry people called ACLU's office in Chicago to demand more information about the pending demonstration. Two groups, one in

New York City and the other in Ohio, called often. The New York contingent, represented on the telephone by a particularly belligerent woman, sought two kinds of information: it wanted to know everything about the planned April 20 demonstration, and it wanted to know what rights it would have in a counterdemonstration.

I took some considerable pleasure in relating to the woman her rights, because I pointed out in each and every available instance that her rights were exactly the same as Frank Collin's. However delightful it was to thus needle the lady, it was also truly bizarre: we were engaged in an extended argument over a demonstration which was not going to take place. The New York group and the Ohio contingent continued to call until the April 20 nondemon stration did not take place. The woman in New York told me, at one point, that she was in the process of chartering buses to bring her counterdemonstrators to Skokie; either she was bluffing or she had been driven to distracted turmoil by a lousy news tip.

In March, as well, came something akin to sensationalism on the local television outlet, which was airing "Holocaust," the television movie about the persecution of Jews under Hitler. When the fictional, fearfully realistic movie paused for commercials and other interruptions, the local NBC affiliate sometimes inserted a "teaser" for the news that told of a coming Skokie story ("Jewish Groups Will Confront Nazi in Skokie – Details at 10," or the like). The consequent blurring of the issues angered several Chicago-area Jews enough to prompt them to call on each local station to tone down the coverage of the controversy.

"Holocaust," however ill used it was by the NBC affiliate, served a purpose in the controversy itself. In a subtle but important way, the airing of the movie at once destroyed the last vestiges of logic in the "menticide" theory; at the same time, the presentation of the film lent substantial merit to Judge Decker's claim that a workable definition of "group libel" was impossible to create.

If the presentation of the symbols of nazism before an audience that contained survivors was, as the survivor litigation asserted, a tort, then surely "Holocaust" caused that tort. While it could be argued that the intent was different in the two cases, it could also be fairly argued that, intent aside, the creators of the movie had done their absolute best to re-create the horrors, traumas, emotions, and feelings of the actual holocaust. Whatever the intent, the harm from Collin's presentation of the symbol could certainly be no worse than the harm from a graphic, historically sensitive re-creation of the crimes committed under that symbol.

As Abbott Rosen of the ADL discovered in a debate on a university campus in southern Illinois, that logic led directly to the prior censorship of the movie. Although Rosen did his best to distinguish Collin from the film, the audience responded by voting, overwhelmingly, in favor of a pure First Amendment position (no censorship) when they were polled at the end of the evening.

At the same time, Judge Decker's insistence that there could be no valid way to define group libel took on greater stature with each evening's airing of the movie. The realistic portrayal of Nazi officers engaged in anti-Semitic crimes could surely be said to foster — if only in a few misguided citizens — anti-Semitism itself. The libel of nazism was running in prime time on national television as Judge Decker issued his opinion suggesting that a "group libel" law would sweep much too broadly. It seemed perfectly plausible, as Decker's ruling suggested, that a well-intentioned, zealous attorney could oppose "Holocaust" on the basis of group libel as easily as he could Frank Collin.

Even without the subtleties of group libel law raised by "Holocaust," the media had their hands full. The local journalists skipped from one new development to the next. As soon as Sol Goldstein's call for a massive confrontation in Skokie had disappeared from the front pages, the JDL announced that they would also confront Collin with a single objective, to "bust heads," while an increasing number of reporters from outside the immediate Chicago area tried to write one up-to-date, comprehensive Skokie story.

By now, my bare-bones, facts-only background report for journalists could take up to half an hour to recite. Since an increasing number of journalists were calling for the first time because their editors were no longer content to use wire-service copy, the hours of the day filled with press conversations seemed to grow and grow. The frustration grew as well, for I knew that most of what I was providing as background would not even get into the background of the stories. The enormous amount of information that now attended the controversy had outstripped the available space for it in columns of print or air time.

Inevitably, under those circumstances, the public was ill informed. The legal points in dispute were as often as not reduced to a single paragraph in many stories; Collin's actual plan for his demonstration continued to be reported in a word or two; the complete history of the litigation might be given a sentence. In fairness, such superficial attention to some of the facts in the controversy was all that was possible, for the events in the federal court at the time were more than enough to keep even the most conscientious and diligent reporter busy.

Shortly after Judge Decker's decision was rendered, ACLU had petitioned him for an end to the forty-five-day stay he had imposed on his own judgment. It was our contention that Decker had, in fact, read the law properly, that prior restraint was both inappropriate and unconstitutional, and that the stay constituted still more prior restraint. Skokie rebutted by arguing that Decker's reservations about group libel were well founded and that it would be a tragedy if Decker allowed Collin to demonstrate only to have an appeals court find, after the fact, that the Skokie group libel law was valid.

Judge Decker refused to lift the stay of his order on March 17. Shortly thereafter, David Goldberger took the same question to the next highest court, the Seventh Circuit Court of Appeals. There David presented to a three-judge panel his contention that the stay was unconstitutional prior restraint. On March 31, the circuit panel denied the motion to lift the stay. Although that action left the restraint in force, the panel scheduled the case itself for argument, thus ensuring that the restraint would be short-lived.

The speed with which the federal judiciary responded to the issue of continuing prior restraint ought to have stood as an object lesson for the Illinois courts. What followed, however, put the Illinois courts to shame.

The seventh circuit (like each such circuit court within the federal system) is composed of a panel of judges from which is selected a smaller three-judge court for each case to be heard. On April 6, in an extraordinary move, the entire seventh circuit court convened a hearing to review the matter of the stay.

The entire circuit court overruled the three-judge panel it had assigned to the case. The stay of Judge Decker's ruling was lifted, while, at the same time, the full circuit scheduled a greatly compressed calendar for the case itself. In one sweeping blow, the court's judges had eradicated an unconstitutional prior restraint and scheduled (for exactly eight days hence) a full hearing on the appeal of Decker's decision. There was no mistaking the intent of the court: prior restraint would not be tolerated nor would any case involving it be allowed to languish.

It had taken the Illinois courts an entire summer just to leave prior restraint in force and the remainder of the year to lift it; in the space of a mere month, a similar case of prior restraint had gone through most of the federal judiciary and received expedited care all the way. What made the contrast between the two reactions all the more stark was the astonishing fact that the seventh circuit judges had acted *without being asked to do so*.

David Goldberger, although convinced that the three-judge panel had acted improperly in upholding Decker's stay, had not petitioned the full circuit for relief. Skokie had not petitioned for relief from the stay, of course, because Skokie did not want relief. The seventh circuit judges acted on their own initiative, presumably compelled by the gravity of the First Amendment issues and the import of continued prior restraint on political speech. By comparison, the Illinois judicial performance seemed even more grossly languid and legally indefensible.

As one form of prior restraint fell before the seventh circuit, another form of prior restraint arose in an entirely different forum. Several legislators, in response to pressure from citizens in Skokie, introduced in the Illinois legislature two bills which, if passed and enacted, would create a state law similar in most respects to Skokie's group libel ordinance and which would also stop Collin, in advance, from demonstrating. The measures passed the Illinois Senate on May 3, raising the very real possibility of still more restraint and still more litigation against it.

Frank Collin took instant notice of the legislation. As soon as it had passed the Senate, he began to renew his calls for "white free speech," insisting that all he had ever wanted was to air his views in Marquette Park and that the legislation was still further evidence of a conspiracy to prevent that airing. That Collin reacted to the bills from a Marquette Park frame of reference only reinforced the ambiguity of his plans for Skokie. Whatever impact the bills might eventually have on the broad controversy, Collin's reaction to them provided still further evidence that he was entertaining second thoughts about his plan to go to the suburbs.

The pressure of the controversy had shifted. Where Skokie had been pressed to excessive limits to prevent Collin from coming, now Collin was under considerable pressure to make good his threat. As each new court ruling put Collin closer to the village, Collin himself had to confront the obvious fact that Skokie probably could not stop him. If all the barriers came down, as they seemed likely to, then Frank Collin would, after all, face Skokie. The illusion was confronting reality.

159

The appeal that Skokie's lawyers took from Judge Decker's finding that all three ordinances were unconstitutional was decided on May 22, 1978. The United States Court of Appeals for the Seventh Circuit affirmed, in every respect, Judge Decker's finding and ordered the Village of Skokie to issue a demonstration permit to Frank Collin and the National Socialist Party of America.

The circuit panel of three judges agreed with Judge Decker right down the line. They affirmed his finding that the insurance ordinance was unconstitutional; they agreed that the ban on uniforms was unlawful; and they held the law of *Beauharnais* (which made group libel a crime) to be invalid and inapplicable to Collin's plan in any event. In supporting Judge Decker, the circuit panel said that even *Beauharnais* required proof that the group libel would lead to some illicit action; the panel agreed with Decker that Skokie had never proved (and could not prove in advance) that such action would take place. Thus, the circuit court held that the case involved pure advocacy, and pure advocacy enjoys the absolute protection of the First Amendment.

Skokie's lawyers announced their intention to appeal the ruling to the United States Supreme Court at the same time they said that, without question, they would obey the order of the court and issue the permit to Frank Collin. In public, David and I reacted to the ruling positively; in private, we realized almost as soon as we had read the ruling that Skokie could not possibly prevail in the Supreme Court. The circuit's language, like Judge Decker's, left absolutely no room for an appeal of any sort, much less a successful one.

The various Jewish organizations affirmed their intentions to confront Collin in Skokie. Rumors of a counter-demonstration were spreading — it would number in the tens of thousands, a major contingent of congressmen was planning to attend, jumbo jets were being chartered for transportation, the Governor of Illinois would (or would not) attend — and with the ruling of the circuit court the air of expectancy surrounding the coming confrontation grew ever more thick.

Richard Salem and Werner Petterson called our office in the wake of the ruling. The two Justice Department officials first wanted to be sure that they understood the ruling; once they were sure of its content, they speculated as to whether Collin would go to Skokie or not. Their patient neutrality — and their access to Skokie's officials, ACLU, and Collin — had led them to see with some clarity Collin's wavering position. Both men seemed to think they could capitalize on it and avoid the confrontation.

The attention of the public, through the media, was not focused on ACLU or the Justice Department's Community Relations Service agents or even, particularly, on the Jewish reaction to the most recent court ruling. The attention of the media — and to a very real extent the attention of a large portion of the world — was focused on Frank Collin.

Frank Collin, at last, stood face to face with the Village of Skokie. There remained, with the circuit court ruling, absolutely no legal barrier whatsoever to Collin's planned demonstration. A permit was forthcoming, in fact, which would guarantee Frank Collin the protected right to appear on the steps of the village hall in Skokie, Illinois, on Sunday, June 25, 1978.

161

8

Only Collin Lost

On May 23, 1978, standing squarely in the center of the path leading directly to Skokie, Frank Collin turned and marched in the opposite direction. He couched his decision in terms which he must have thought face-saving, and he did not entirely eliminate the possibility of a demonstration in Skokie. Nevertheless, Collin made it quite clear to anyone interested that he would much prefer not to demonstrate in Skokie.

Collin told reporters that his objective, from the very beginning of the controversy, had been to get back into Marquette Park. He had never really wanted to go to Skokie at all, Collin said, so he was now perfectly willing to give up his planned demonstration there if three conditions were met. First, Collin said that no further legal barriers could be erected to stop his Skokie demonstration; the other side of that coin, an affirmation of his existing right to go to Skokie, would also be acceptable. Second, Collin demanded that the two bills currently before the Illinois House be defeated. Finally, Collin asked that his right to demonstrate in Marquette Park be specifically restored.

Collin's offer certainly suggested that the man believed his own illusion, for, if nothing else, it had a remarkable arrogance. He was asking that federal court proceedings

163

be guaranteed in advance, that the Chicago Park District give up or lose its struggle over the insurance requirement, and that a legislative forum agree to his request. However grand the illusion, it still held power, for the arrogance of Collin's offer was far less a matter of concern than the substance of it. In particular, Richard Salem and Werner Petterson took Collin's offer very seriously.

On May 26, amid the swirl of court rulings, incessant press coverage, the increasing likelihood of a massive counterdemonstration, and the accumulated tension of more than a year of sustained controversy, David and I sat down to a meeting with Salem and Petterson. Although we began on common ground, it was a most frustrating encounter.

At our morning meeting we agreed that Frank Collin would, eventually, have the unfettered right to demonstrate in Skokie. All four of us shared the solid conviction that Skokie's legal defenses were now useless and we also agreed (Salem emphatically, David and I less so) that the legislation in Springfield seemed unlikely to pass both the House and the Governor's scrutiny. From that point, however, we departed.

David and I had spent some considerable time in the days after Judge Decker's ruling discussing Collin's demonstration. Although the public at large seemed willing to believe that Collin would bail out of his stated plan, David and I reminded each other that Frank Collin had taken his followers to Skokie's border in April of the previous year. The prospect that Collin might very well carry out his plan troubled us greatly.

We both felt that the principles at stake in the legal controversy, which we had fought so hard to protect,

164

could all too easily explode if Collin actually demonstrated and anything—anything at all—went wrong. The law and logic both dictated that Skokie's officials had new and enormous responsibilities: they would have to protect lawful First Amendment activity for both Collin and the counterdemonstrators while at the same time maintain the peace. It was, to say the least, a tall order.

David and I firmly believed that Skokie's failure to uphold any one of those responsibilities would lead to serious trouble. If, for example, Skokie allowed the Nazi demonstration to go forward without holding the audience at a safe distance, all hell would be sure to break loose. If that happened, the precious victories that the First Amendment had finally enjoyed would not mean a damn thing, for all of Skokie's fears would be realized and the law would turn to mush.

Our concern was considerable. Although we knew, for a certainty, that the crowds had to be controlled, we also knew that both sides had an absolute right to air their views. There would be an enormous crowd in Skokie on June 25 by even the most modest estimates, and as sure as we were of the First Amendment law governing that fact, neither David nor I had the faintest idea what such a crowd would demand of the law enforcement officials of Skokie. Because we wanted to be able to evaluate, at least in rudimentary terms, Skokie's law enforcement plans, Goldberger and I went to lunch (before our meeting with Salem and Petterson) with a highly experienced senior officer of the Chicago Police Department.

The officer is a long-time cop, a veteran of years of experience on Chicago's force. He was, among other things, a command-level officer in Chicago's Loop for several years in the aftermath of the 1968 Democratic Convention. In those hectic days, David had been a principal advocate of the First Amendment rights of demonstrators other than Frank Collin, and he had often encountered this particular officer. David had grown to respect the man, and out of that respect he asked if we could lunch with him to discuss our concerns about the demonstration in Skokie.

The officer instructed us well. The more he talked about crowd control, the more uneasy David and I became.

"What are they doing about the press?" the cop asked. "That's a good barometer. If they're on top of the press, they've probably got good sense.

"We used to send our guys into demonstrations under-cover. Everybody *knew* who they were, they stuck out like sore thumbs. We wanted them to stick out, of course; we wanted people to know that the cops were every-where.

"You've got to plan all sorts of escape routes. You've got to be able to get the troublemakers out of the area quickly."

The officer seemed sure that Skokie's problems would not include manpower. He said there was little doubt about the village's ability to marshal forces, but that the key was not numbers but planning.

Our reading of Skokie's plans for the demonstration, by late May, was decidedly disquieting. The basic steps seemed to have been taken. There were, indeed, lots of back-up resources available to the village, and Skokie's officials had sited the counterdemonstration on a high school campus some distance from the village hall. Still, the reports we were getting suggested that a crisp, clean effort was not taking place. Among other things, we were hearing reports of conflict among the various law enforcement agencies, rumors of ego clashes and lack of cooperation.

So David and I came to our meeting with the two Justice Department negotiators with grave concerns about the prospect for a lawful encounter on June 25. Petterson and Salem came, instead, with an abiding interest in avoiding the encounter altogether. Since they viewed the actual confrontation as something to avoid, they appeared to relegate planning for that confrontation to a decidedly secondary status.

I was extremely frustrated with both men as soon as the meeting began. I was sincerely angry at their seeming disinterest in the potential for trouble in Skokie, but I was far angrier at their dispassionate approach to the issues. After more than a year of sustained battling, I found that I could not deal effectively with two men who stood neither with Skokie nor ACLU. In my world, there had ceased to be room for anybody who was not "for" or "against."

In spite of me, Salem and Petterson did the job they had come to my office to do. They carefully, patiently, and thoroughly explored every aspect of Frank Collin's now public "offer" to stay out of Skokie. Once we had all agreed about the prospects in the Skokie-related litigation, the two mediators had only two remaining questions. First, they needed to know if the litigation surrounding Marquette Park and the Chicago Park District's insurance requirement might lead to Collin's having access to that park; second, they wanted to know if Frank Collin might be interested in another demonstration site if Marquette remained unavailable.

Neither David nor I could answer the second question. We had, throughout the controversy, maintained our distance from Collin. As his legal counsel, David advised Collin on matters pertaining directly to the litigation and nothing more; I continued to have little contact with Collin, although I was by now accustomed to dealing with him by telephone. We could not answer any question about Collin's plans, because we were not able to. We had no control over his demonstrations; we had not and would not advise him about those demonstrations; we had not and would not counsel him on anything other than his constitutional rights. If Salem and Petterson wanted to know if Collin had an interest in yet another demonstration site, they would have to ask him directly.

Of Marquette Park and the Chicago Park District litigation we knew a great deal, of course, and David went over the early history of that suit with the two men. He then summarized the sorry record of evasion that had held Collin out of the parks since July 1977; to that sorry record there was now yet another entry.

Frank Collin had applied for another Marquette Park permit early in the spring. It was that application, delayed by the weather, which Richard Troy had assured Judge Leighton in September would encounter no problems. To absolutely nobody's surprise, there were problems galore.

Not only did Collin discover that the sixty-thousand-dollar insurance requirement was still in force, he also found that another barrier had been erected as well. This time, the insurance requirement was paired with another ground for refusing the permit application: the

Chicago Park District said that, since Frank Collin's organization was not registered with the Secretary of State, he was not qualified for a permit.

By the time Salem and Petterson came to our office to discuss *Collin* v. *O'Malley,* Judge Leighton's order in that case had been cited by Judge Decker in the Skokie case and it *still* had not been obeyed by the park district. David Goldberger had concluded, before the meeting on May 26, that the only way to stop the continuing abuse of the First Amendment by the park district's officials was to try to have them cited for contempt in Judge Leighton's court. Such a motion was already in preparation when Salem and Petterson asked about Collin's chances of gaining access to Marquette Park, and it was filed with the court the next day.

David told the two men that he could not, of course, guarantee the outcome of the hearing on his motion; he also said that he (and Judge Decker) believed that the language of Leighton's ruling was clear enough and that Leighton was likely to force the park district to cease its ducking and dodging and obey the order.

The meeting ended, then, with Salem and Petterson optimistic about the potential for avoiding a demonstration by Collin in Skokie. It seemed to both men that each of the three conditions Collin had cited would be met (although nobody in the room believed for a moment that Collin's citing of them had anything to do with their accomplishment), and there remained the additional possibility that Collin might be interested in a new site as well.

On June 1, Frank Collin came to ACLU, where he joined Werner Petterson, Richard Salem, David Goldberger,

169

and me for a meeting. There had been two additional developments in the four days between the two meetings with the mediators in my office, and each had been attended by still more news coverage and a further deepening of the resolve of Collin's opponents in and out of Skokie to confront him there, so the tension was, if possible, still greater. On May 30, Skokie had issued to Frank Collin a permit for a demonstration at the village hall on June 25; on May 31, Skokie had petitioned the United States Supreme Court for a stay of the circuit ruling, a stay which would halt the now permitted demonstration.

Richard Salem talked at length to Frank Collin. Salem did not in any way put pressure on Collin to stay out of Skokie; rather, he simply focused Collin's attention on those pressures which already existed. Collin, now face to face with his own plan, listened as Salem described, among other things, the very real physical dangers which existed. Collin himself had heard the JDL's threats, and he knew of the growing size of the demonstration being organized against him. He also knew from news reports that a massive police force was being prepared. Richard Salem did not have to mention any of those factors specifically to convince Collin that it was dangerous to go to Skokie.

Salem then reinforced Collin's stated desire to stay away, largely by assuring Collin, as best he could, that the three conditions seemed likely to be met. Salem did not guarantee anything at all, of course, but he told Collin that it seemed most probable that the courts would continue to uphold his right to go to Skokie, that the legislation would not pass into law, and that (sooner or later) Collin would probably win his suit to get back into Marquette Park. Collin responded, in his most officious tones, that he had never really meant to go to Skokie and that if the conditions were met, he would not promise *never* to go, but he would give up his immediate plans to do so.

Salem then put to Collin a surprising proposition: it was, Salem said, possible that one of the three conditions might not be met, or that the access to Marquette Park could take some time to gain; would Collin be interested in an alternate site for a demonstration? Frank Collin said yes. Instantly, Salem began to suggest that Collin had solved the problem. If another site could be found, the confrontation could be avoided.

In the discussion that followed, Salem and Petterson together hammered away at the wisdom of demonstrating elsewhere than in Skokie, and they also drew from David and me a list of places where people in Chicago demonstrate. Somebody suggested the plaza outside the federal court building. Collin liked that idea and Salem closed in; before I quite realized what had happened, Collin had traded Skokie for the Federal Plaza.

There is absolutely nothing special about a demonstration on the Federal Plaza in Chicago. Anyone wishing to assemble there is free to do so at virtually any time. Frank Collin, for example, could have taken his small band to that site on almost any day during the entire Skokie controversy. In the space of less than two hours, however, Collin had traded his hard-won right to a highly visible demonstration in Skokie for a demonstration he could have had at any time for the asking.

I do not believe that Salem and Petterson tricked

Frank Collin, although I believe they did a masterful job of leading him along. Frank Collin, before he entered the meeting with those two men, was fully aware of the enormous reaction he would generate in Skokie; the thought of snipers alone must have chilled him often. Even if Collin was willing to face that danger, there were new rumors floating through the city that he might very well have to do so with very few, if any, of his followers. A local journalist reported that a source within Collin's group was saying that many of his followers did not have any intention of marching in Skokie, Illinois. For Collin, then, the thought of actually going to Skokie held significant humiliation at best and physical dangers, which realistically included his own death, at worst.

By June 1, Frank Collin had given up any thought of going to Skokie.

Although it did not matter at all, each of Frank Collin's three conditions were met in the time it took him to arrange for a short demonstration on the Federal Plaza in Chicago's Loop. Collin gave up his Skokie demonstration on June 1 (or, perhaps, sometime before then); his three conditions were met by the twentieth.

On June 6, the House Judiciary Committee in Springfield heard testimony on the two bills proposing new "group libel" laws for Illinois. The principal proponent of the measure before the committee was a lawyer representing one of the organized Jewish groups of Chicago; the principal opponent was Aryeh Neier, ACLU's national executive director, who had flown in from New York to testify. The committee, which engaged in a most spirited debate, voted to recommend the defeat of both bills.

On June 12, the United States Supreme Court, by a

172

margin of seven justices in support, two in dissent, refused to grant a stay of the Seventh Circuit Court's ruling. The Court thus struck down the Village of Skokie's last legal weapon. There, at last, the main Skokie cases rested; the highest court in the land had refused to stop Frank Collin's demonstration.

The next day, on the thirteenth, the full Illinois House of Representatives defeated both group libel measures.

On June 20, in response to ACLU's motion, Judge George Leighton ordered the Chicago Park District to issue to Frank Collin a permit to demonstrate in Marquette Park on July 9, 1978. Leighton did not hold the park district in contempt, but he made it quite clear that the park district was under a direct order to issue the permit.

There were two final, futile legal assaults against Collin's Skokie demonstration. On June 15, Jerome Torshen, who had already failed to get his case reheard by the Illinois Supreme Court, filed an emergency petition with U.S. Supreme Court Justice John Paul Stevens. On behalf of Sol Goldstein and other holocaust survivors, Torshen asked Stevens to halt the pending demonstration until the survivors' case could be heard by the full Supreme Court. On June 20, Mr. Justice Stevens denied the request; Torshen promptly filed the same petition with Justice William Rehnquist, who also denied it. There, without ever having a single substantive hearing, the "menticide" litigation ended.

At roughly the same time, a brand-new suit was filed against Frank Collin. A gentleman named Black, who resided at the time in Niles Township, a subdivision of Skokie, sued the Village of Skokie for issuing an invalid

permit to Frank Collin. Black's contention was that
Collin was not registered with the Secretary of State
and that the permit issued to him was therefore invalid.
While Skokie's lawyer, Harvey Schwartz, stood uncom-
fortably mute, David Goldberger patiently explained to
the Cook County judge on the case that if he forced
Schwartz to revoke the permit, he would instantly put
Schwartz in contempt of the order of the court of appeals.
That was enough to prevent the judge from providing
Skokie with a last-minute reprieve, and the case was
dismissed.

On June 24, a bright Saturday almost fourteen months
after the Village of Skokie first took Frank Collin to
court, the Neo-Nazi leader assembled a bare handful of
his followers at his southwest Chicago headquarters. For
obvious reasons of security, the Chicago police dictated
Collin's every move. The Neo-Nazis were loaded into a police
van and transported to the Federal Plaza in downtown
Chicago. Moving quickly and carefully, the police escorted
Collin and his followers through the basement of the
Federal Building and out onto the concrete plaza.

Frank Collin and his followers marched onto the plaza
through a corridor of uniformed Chicago police, emerging
on the plaza itself to face a crowd of several thousand
seething, furious, scream-distorted faces. Although he
had a portable amplifier, Collin could not be heard at
all; the ceaseless angry roar made whatever Collin said
impossible to hear. The demonstration lasted no more
than fifteen or twenty minutes. Frank Collin and his
followers left the plaza and returned to their headquarters
under heavy police guard all the way.

On Sunday, June 25, Frank Collin did not exercise his court-mandated First Amendment right to appear on the steps of the village hall in Skokie.

On July 9, after Richard Troy had tried without success to get both the Seventh Circuit Court of Appeals and the Supreme Court to stop the demonstration, Frank Collin led a demonstration in Marquette Park. Again, he faced a huge hostile audience and again his message was inaudible for the cries of opposition.

The First Amendment to the United States Constitution *is* democracy. It protects Frank Collin's right to express his ideas in order that everyone may examine those ideas and accept or reject them.

If Frank Collin had political power—if he were, for example, in control of a community such as Skokie—Frank Collin would censor those ideas with which he disagrees and he would protect the ideas he supports. That concept is the cornerstone of fascism and the antithesis of free speech.

Political censorship is no better a theory of government when Frank Collin advocates it than it is when put into practice by the Village of Skokie or the Chicago Park District or holocaust survivors. Whether it comes wrapped in a swastika or an American flag, political censorship merits only rejection.

That rejection took place in the courts which reviewed the Skokie litigation. Although an alarming proportion of the judges who heard the various cases lacked the courage to honor the law, it is nevertheless true that the law was ultimately honored. Frank Collin secured from the courts of America a firm, forthright affirmation of the very idea his own doctrine cannot tolerate: the Fascist won ringing victories for freedom of speech.

The rejection took place, as well, in the streets. The body politic, which had for so long been fooled by Collin's remarkable illusion, eventually saw the truth. Frank Collin's audience watched as he loaded his "army" of storm-troopers into the back of a single police van, and his audience also watched as he faced a wall of citizens, layer upon layer thick, which rose in determined opposition to all that Collin represents.

Frank Collin's audience had looked beyond the decep-tive symbols and discovered, at last, that beyond those symbols lay a mere coward. Frank Collin was willing to taunt his enemies from afar or from behind the protection of uniformed police, but he had not the courage to carry out his own threats. Once Collin stepped into the light and the illusion fell away, there was a single, inevitable response: the roar of rejection drowned out Frank Collin's very words.

Only Frank Collin lost. The survivor community of Skokie and the broader community of Jews in Greater Chicago must surely have taken comfort in the security which tens of thousands of citizens were prepared to provide. Skokie's officials had lost their court battles, but they had certainly responded, win or lose, to the expressed desires of their constituency, and that is, after all, precisely what elected officials are supposed to do.

The American Civil Liberties Union is now nearly as large as it was before the controversy. In the immediate wake of the damage, some special fund-raising efforts and the outpouring of extra support from members who

176

had remained with the organization (an outpouring which came in response to a compelling letter from David Goldberger) eradicated most of the short-term damage. Over the long term, ACLU will surely profit — if only from the internal strength it found — for having insisted that free speech means free speech.

In the last days of the Skokie controversy, David and I held a press conference in the ACLU office. In addition to reporters from around the nation and at least two foreign camera crews, the conference was attended by many local reporters. Among them was a woman who had covered the story of the Neo-Nazis and Skokie off and on from the beginning. The woman raised her hand to ask a question, and David called for it.

"Frank Collin says that if he has trouble getting into Marquette Park again, he might want to march in Skokie," the woman said. *"Is that legal?"*

Although the question portrayed, almost to perfection, the confusion which had attended the coverage of the controversy from the beginning, not even the confusion of the media could obscure the answer.

The answer — the powerful, lawful, majestically strong answer — is Yes.

Epilogue

Frank Collin generated some attention from the press and the public only twice more after his brief demonstrations in Chicago. On the first occasion, several months after the Marquette Park demonstration, it was reported that Collin had threatened a suburb of Cleveland in the same way he had threatened Skokie. The press accounts of that incident suggest that Collin was simply ignored, but only after the laughter had died down. Collin returned to Chicago without further word.

In early 1980, the media in Chicago reported that Frank Collin had been arrested by Chicago's police on a morals charge involving the taking of indecent liberties with under-aged boys. Collin was tried on those charges and convicted. He was sentenced to seven years in an Illinois prison and began serving that sentence immediately. At about the same time, Collin was thrown out of the National Socialist Party of America.

The Village of Skokie remains virtually the same, unchanged for all of the turmoil which rocked it.

In October 1978 I resigned as director of ACLU in Illinois to recover from battle fatigue and to write. David Goldberger remained with ACLU for two more years and in that time he reaped richly deserved recognition from his peers in the legal community and enjoyed as well numerous tributes to his work from schools and organizations. David remains in the arena of civil liberties — he now teaches future lawyers how to protect basic freedoms.

The First Amendment is still as strong as ever, perhaps even stronger.

Index

Index

Index

Roger Baldwin Foundation, 132
Rosen, Abbott, 155; and *Goldstein* v. *Collin*, 106, 107, 110, 111, 114–115
Rothschild, Edwin, 50, 82–83
Royko, Mike, 7

Salem, Richard, 151, 161; meeting with ACLU members, 164–169; meeting with Collin, 169–172
Schwartz, Harvey, 32, 34, 101, 141, 142, 174; and *Skokie* v. *Collin*, 38, 60; and *Goldstein* v. *Collin*, 114
Skokie, Illinois: description of, 25–27, 179; initial reaction to Collin's request to demonstrate, 27–32; village council's plan to deal with Collin, 32–35; Jewish population's reaction to Collin, 35–38; *Skokie* v. *Collin*, 38–39, 53–62, 94–97, 135–137; Collin's attempt to demonstrate in, 71–76; ordinances passed by council to stop Collin, 76–79, 84; reaction to Supreme Court ruling on Collin, 87; Hamlin's speaking engagement in, 101–103; court rulings against three ordinances of, 146–150, 157–158, 160; contacting of Community Relations Service, 151; public plans to counterdemonstrate in, 152; Collin's conditions for giving up demonstrating in, 163–164; Collin's agreement to not demonstrate in, 170–172
Skokie v. *Collin*, 53–62; public reaction to, 64–70
Smith, Mayor Albert, 32, 34, 59, 60, 141

Stevens, Justice John Paul, 86, 173
Sullivan, Judge Harold, 73, 74–75, 80
Survivor litigation, *see* Goldstein

Tenth Illinois Congressional District, 26–27
Thomson, Meldrim, 41
Torshen, Jerome, and *Goldstein* v. *Collin*, 108, 110, 113, 114–115, 173
Troy, Richard, 21–22, 139–140, 168, 175

United States Court of Appeals for the Seventh Circuit, ruling on *Collin* v. *Skokie*, 157–158, 160
United States District Court: preliminary order in *Collin* v. *O'Malley* insurance requirement, 139; ruling on *Collin* v. *Skokie*, 146–150
United States Supreme Court: ruling on *Skokie* v. *Collin*, 86–87, 90; Illinois judiciary's reaction to ruling of, 93, 96; ruling on group libel, 149
Urban League, 10

Weisman, Sydney, 69, 103
Wosik, Judge Joseph, 53–54, 75–76, 79–80, 85, 96; bias against Collin, 54–57, 62, 63; ruling of Skokie case back to, 96; and *Goldstein* v. *Collin*, 116